KLEIN DYTHAM
ARCHITECTURE

to TOKYO and BEYOND

Foreword by Toyo Ito // Introduction by Amy Frearson

images Publishing

Contents

Thoughtful Design Inspires Fun and Joy

Toyo Ito

Astrid Klein and Mark Dytham, founders of Klein Dytham architecture (KDa), came to my office in 1988 during their first visit to Japan. They had just graduated from the Royal College of Art in London and I was impressed by the beautiful presentation of their diploma projects. After traveling around the country, they visited me again, this time expressing an enthusiasm for and desire to work in Japan. At that time, we didn't have much work to offer them, but I remembered that a close friend had requested an interior renovation for a beauty salon. So, with the client's permission, I entrusted the project to them. It was probably their first project, but they completed it to perfection. The client was so pleased that she asked them to work on another job for her.

After 2 years as staff at my firm, Astrid and Mark established Klein Dytham architecture in 1991. Yukinari Hisayama joined them in 1996. Despite many challenges, they have continued to thrive for more than 30 years.

Most of KDa's projects are commercial buildings. One reason for this is their hospitality-oriented approach to architecture. This must not be mistaken for pandering to clients. Instead it's based on their philosophy that architecture should always bring fun, joy and pleasure to people.

Japan's national and local authorities also rarely accept foreign architectural teams for public building design. Language barriers are one reason but, more significantly, municipalities in Japan want to avoid what they perceive as inconvenient communication and discussion. In other words, they are less interested in architectural ideas than in budgets and construction deadlines. They prefer to work with organizations that will simply toe the line.

When I see countries like China, South Korea, Singapore and Taiwan inviting foreign firms to participate in design competitions, I can't help but feel that Japan suffers some cultural impoverishment. Yet, despite these circumstances, KDa's positive attitude prevails with bright and joyful creations, which is something that is truly admirable.

This pursuit of fun and joy is reflected in KDa's projects. The louver-like façades of Ginza Place (2016) and Daikanyama T-SITE (2011), for example, combine GRC units to resemble woven textiles. To passersby, the pattern of Ginza Place creates an illusion of a 3D curved surface. For Daikanyama T-SITE, the repetition of the brand's T-shaped logo forms a distinctive façade. The designs bring a fresh, lively expression to streets dominated by buildings of glass and metal.

This is true for other KDa projects—their designs are consistently smart and witty, without any sense of excessive expression tainted by commercialism.

In Bangkok, a similar façade concept is more delicately realized for the interiors of Open House, a complex including a bookstore, several restaurants and cafes designed in 2017. Its landscape of box-like structures, clad with wooden fretwork and positioned like islands in a vast interior, is incredibly beautiful. Combined with countless leaf prints across the ceiling, the project creates a cool atmosphere within the hot streets of Bangkok. It's a project that also conveys KDa's refined sense of style.

Many of KDa's designs, like Open House, feature nature as a motif. PokoPoko (2019) and Leaf Chapel (2004), both designed for the Japanese developer Hoshino Resorts, blend into their lush natural surroundings. PokoPoko's three wooden huts are connected by conical roofs of varying slopes, each with skylights tilted at different angles. Their unexpected appearance in the forest reveals a sense of humor and playfulness. The petite, dome-shaped Leaf Chapel is also within a forest. Small perforations in its exterior steel sheath form constellation-like plant patterns. Both the projects evoke fantasy, as if transporting us into a fairy-tale world.

Such designs seem to stem from a desire to express the joy and happiness of living. Perhaps this reflects KDa's own aspirations to make everyday life fun and full of joy.

KDa is also involved in various creative activities beyond its design work, most notably its PechaKucha Night presentation platform. This series of simple events invites young architects, designers and artists to present and talk about twenty images for 20 seconds each. Since it launched in 2003, it has been held in more than 1300 cities worldwide for more than 20 years. The sustaining energy behind this is remarkable. It's an activity that symbolizes KDa's determination to globally connect and communicate, transcending cultural and societal differences.

Every year, Japan experiences significant damage from natural disasters—earthquakes, typhoons, heavy rains. The Great East Japan Earthquake and its ensuing tsunami and nuclear power plant disaster of 2011 were particularly devastating. Many locals in Tohoku coastal towns lost their homes or were forced to evacuate. To support these people and help restore their communities, we began an initiative to provide small wooden community-use huts called Home-for-All, and KDa was actively involved in these efforts. Its Home-for-All for Children built in a park in Soma City, Fukushima Prefecture, was designed as an indoor playground for small children who were unable to play outside due to fears of possible radiation. The circular, dome-shaped building with tree-like pillars became a lively space for community revival, not just for children, but also for their parents.

After the 2016 Kumamoto earthquakes and the recent Noto Peninsula earthquake, KDa has continued to be involved in support activities as a member of HOME-FOR-ALL, now a nonprofit organization.

In addition to all of KDa's activities, Astrid is a lecturer of the Children's Architecture School, a private educational program that I run. Held twenty times a year, the program invites forty children, aged ten to twelve, to explore themes such as "What is a house?" and "What is a town?" It aims to inspire them to think comprehensively about life, family, society and other topics that are not taught in schools, through sketching and modelling. Astrid's guidance, which follows the educational policy of fostering the imagination to develop as freely as possible, has produced exceptional results. When she teaches, her wonderful sense of color encourages the children's sketches to become vivid and vibrant.

KDa is a unique team, active not just in architecture but in a wide range of fields, from interior design, furniture and graphic design to social activities. Its work continues to inspire courage in organizations and creatives still confined to specific genres.

KDa's Language of Architecture

Amy Frearson

The best buildings communicate without words. You should know instinctively what's great about them, how to move through them, how to behave when you're inside. This is one of the things I learn from Astrid Klein and Mark Dytham as we sit down to discuss their projects from more than 30 years of architectural practice. They dislike signage in buildings, believing the experience of architecture should be completely intuitive. "If you have to rely on signage, your building is not good enough," states Astrid. "The building should be able to do without it, otherwise you haven't done your job."

The idea of architecture as a language resonates with the career journey of this duo, who moved from London to Tokyo immediately after graduating from the Royal College of Art in 1988. Japan is a country where, for various reasons, foreign architects often struggle to compete with native speakers. That's still the case today, let alone in the 1990s. Astrid and Mark succeeded where others failed, despite neither of them speaking any Japanese at first. The communicative nature of their designs saw them smash through the language barrier and never look back. They share the belief that a building should speak in a way that goes beyond function and comfort—it should elicit joy and wonder. "We want our architecture to be about delight," says Mark. "A lot of architecture is way too serious. We're always trying to bring that wry smile."

Astrid and Mark's understanding of each other is key to the success of their partnership, and was apparent from the start. Astrid was born in Italy to German parents, and schooled in France, so she was still getting to grips with English when she enrolled at the Royal College of Art. UK-born Mark recalls being impressed by her work and increasingly acting as her interpreter during critiques. "I could explain her projects better than she could," he says, to which Astrid agrees. "Magically, Mark understood me very well," she adds. It was a telling sign of how their dynamic would strengthen and grow with the launch of their studio, Klein Dytham architecture, in 1991.

KDa's architectural vocabulary expanded with the arrival of Yukinari Hisayama in 1996. Initially an intern, native-speaking Hisa brought a new dimension to Astrid and Mark's ideas. "We were learning from each other," says Mark. Hisa soon became a crucial part of the KDa team, finding a freedom of expression beyond what is typical in a Japanese company hierarchy. He helped the founders learn the subtleties of Japanese humor and wordplay, and even came up with the name PechaKucha, Japanese for 'chit-chat', for their event platform.

I first got to know KDa back in 2012. As the architecture reporter for *Dezeen* magazine, I was tasked with writing a short article about a building the studio had recently completed, Daikanyama T-SITE. Through conversations with Mark, I became intrigued by this clever blend of classic bookshop, lifestyle store, coffee shop and library-esque study space. It was a building that redefined the possibilities of physical retail, targeting the over-fifties by catering to different types of hobby culture across topics including art, fashion, music and travel. It became a career-defining project for KDa, the first of many for the Tsutaya retail chain.

When I finally visited Daikanyama T-SITE in person, in 2023, I found a space that communicates in various ways. The first is with its façade, where custom cladding screens create the sense of a knitted textile.

Look closer and you see it's actually a pattern of interlocking Ts, a subtle but effective reference to the Tsutaya brand identity woven into the architecture. There's more inside, where a "magazine street" naturally directs customers to their area of interest. "We like to think about that journey, as you transition from space to space," says Mark. It's a seamless experience that taps into customer curiosity, encouraging people to explore and linger.

The KDa team have a knack for understanding the mood of the zeitgeist and how it shapes the way we interact with space, from shifting social habits to advancements in technology. In the workplace, the arrival of digital tech at the turn of the century prompted the forward-thinking interior of ad agency Beacon, with its shared workspaces and casual meeting rooms wrapped up in a giant free-flowing ribbon. The studio followed this up with Google's Japan office, where playful graphics and surfaces—including a wall of long blue "hair"—provide workspace zones with distinct characters. But it is in retail where this grasp of human nature really comes to the fore. After the T-SITES came the first flagship store for iconic guitar manufacturer Fender, a brand that previously sold its products exclusively through dealers. Here, KDa crafted a series of moments that immersed visitors in the brand's history and creativity. Spaces are not static like a museum; they facilitate changing displays and invite engagement, resulting in an experience that feels authentic and meaningful.

Underpinning KDa's work is a skill for transforming simple details into moments of delight. This stems in part from the sense of amazement that Astrid and Mark experienced themselves in their early years in Tokyo. "Things that were obvious to the Japanese people were a wonder to us," Astrid remarks. "We like to pick up on that and give it a contemporary twist." One of the ways they do this is by using formal references to tell stories. A restaurant in Atami, famous for its fireworks, features dining pavilions that mimic these colorful displays. A store for audio brand KEF resembles a giant speaker, while a clubhouse at the Risonare Nasu resort looks like a trio of characters wearing tall hats. It's not easy to pull this off without veering into the cartoonish, but KDa's buildings never take it too far. It's a clever tactic for making buildings appear friendlier. "When people recognize things, they feel comfortable," says Astrid. "Architecture shouldn't be hierarchical; it should make you laugh and feel at ease."

To look at KDa's work through the lens of *Learning from Las Vegas*, the seminal 1972 text by Robert Venturi, Denise Scott Brown and Steven Izenour, it could be said to include both ducks and decorated sheds: some buildings communicate through their entire form, while others do so primarily in the façade. Among the most striking of the decorated sheds is Ginza Place, which boasts an articulated skin that appears stretched at the top and squashed at the bottom. Another is the Cartier store in Osaka, where a geometric timber façade could be likened to both precious gems and traditional sake boxes. Mark jokes about how KDa was once described as "glorified graphic designers." While these projects demonstrate an obvious talent for pattern and motif, there is a multidimensionality here that is undeniably architectural. It's a technique that creates brand value in the very fabric of the buildings, a graphic identity that doesn't rely on text or logos.

Over the years, KDa has found different ways of communicating through façades and surfaces. One is the use of digital screens, which opened up the possibility for dynamism. Examples include the Gallery Toto public toilet, with its prerecorded silhouettes giving a false impression of what's happening inside; the Uniqlo Ginza store, with its low-res pixel animations; and the Bloomberg ICE installation, where motion sensors allow visitors to interact with data. In all three, the point of interest is not the tech, but rather the way it facilitates a connection between building and user. "We like to show technology in a different way," says Mark. "It's interesting to do something with a bit more emotion to it." That means the value is not tied to the tech; when it inevitably becomes outdated, that emotional tie remains.

Another emerging theme is the integration of nature, both real and artificial. In addition to living greenery, KDa's designs often make use of nature-inspired iconography. A project for department store Laforet resulted in tree-shaped street furniture, while the Shonan and Kashiwanoha T-SITES feature façades adorned with ivy leaf patterns. Questions around budget and maintenance factored into some of these decisions, but there is also a sense of intention that can't be achieved with plants alone. As Astrid puts it, "If you have the graphic greenery side by side with real greenery, it creates a tension that is a bit more interesting." This was certainly the case with Green Screen, where green walls and nature-inspired graphics combined to create a giant barcode. "By changing the scale of the graphic plants, there was a really nice tension with the real plants," adds Mark.

The KDa founders consider themselves lucky to have arrived on the architectural scene before the emergence of online publishing and social media. Everything changed with the growth of websites like Dezeen and platforms like YouTube and Instagram, which ushered in a generation of architects and designers better versed than their predecessors in communicating ideas to an audience. Astrid, Mark and Hisa were doing this long before it became standard practice; to them, it has always been second nature. "When the building is finished, you can't possibly stand next to it and explain to every passerby what your intentions were; it has to stand for itself," says Astrid. Good timing or not, their achievements are a testament to their ability to speak the language of architecture in a way that anyone can understand and enjoy.

to **TOKYO** ...

"Ginza Place has become a new landmark and gateway to the rejuvenation of Ginza"

GINZA PLACE

Tokyo, Japan // Showrooms, retail, restaurant // 7,350 m²
Sapporo Real Estate // 2016

Ginza Place was designed to engage with its surroundings architecturally and socially. It stands on a corner of one of Tokyo's most famous crossings and takes its cues from local history, traditional culture, and social interaction. Facing the 1932 Seiko House building (formerly the Wako building) and clock tower, its futuristic façade is divided into three distinct sections that echo the horizontal lines of the historical landmark's tripartite structure. Viewed from below, this matching visual axes between the two strikingly different buildings connects the past and present across the bustling intersection.

An architectural innovation in flexible façade and massing, Ginza Place is a landmark for Tokyo's hub of culture and commerce. Its compelling architectural skin—a dynamic design of sleek, white, diamond-shaped panels—complements the district's streets of elegant fashion houses and prestigious galleries.

The proportions of Ginza Place's façade, split by bands of glazing, increase as the building rises. Its three podium floors create a low section of floor-to-ceiling windows, followed by a mid-height section of diamond paneling. Its towering crown extends above the Seiko House clock tower opposite.

Ginza Place's cladding is inspired by *sukashibori*, an intricate openwork technique traditionally used for decorative ceramics and metalwork. Windows hidden within perforations of the façade's design allow light to permeate, while the gradations of its panels give the illusion of fluid convex curves. The façade's lower section panels swell and shrink in size parabolically, as its top section soars upwards, culminating in full-height panels at the building's crown.

More than 5,300 cladding panels were used—each a single sheet of aluminum, scored and folded into prismatic diamonds, welded at the seams, and finished with powder coating. Individually attached, they move independently and resettle when needed, a flexibility requirement of earthquake regulations in Japan.

UBS
SONY
SONY
B.V.D.
FUJIBO
NISSAN
GINZA PLACE

東京メトロ
スパイス
&
ハーブ
お知らせ

なんで、私がペラペラに!?
GINZA CORE
B.V.D.
FUJIBO
SONY
NISSAN
GINZA PLACE
NISSAN
SONY

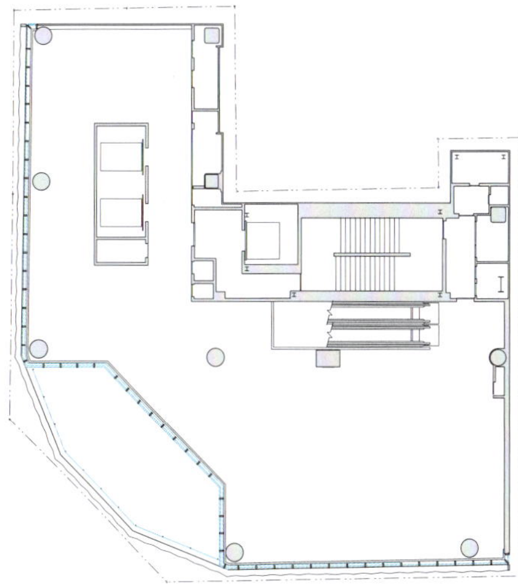

Seventh-floor plan

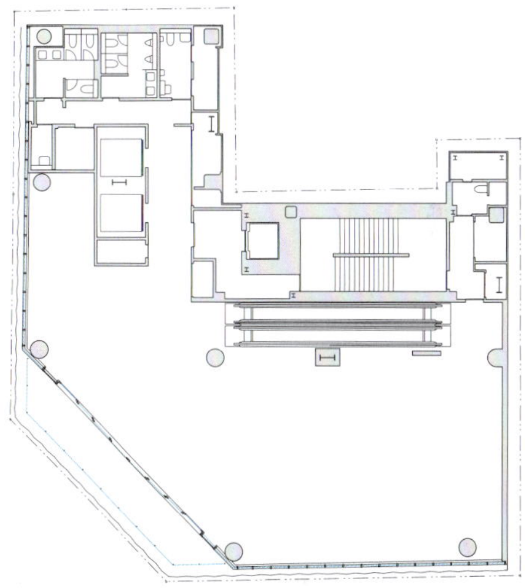

Third-floor plan

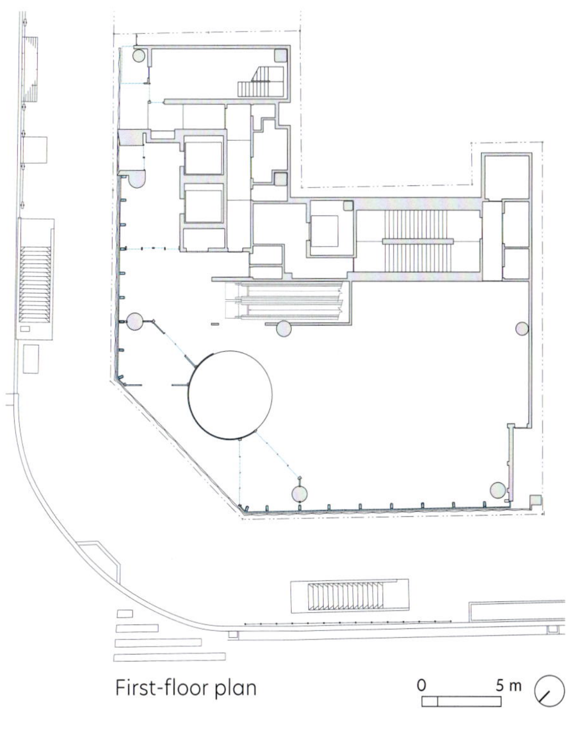

First-floor plan

Jotoshiki

Throughout Japanese history, there have been various ceremonies to commemorate different stages of construction projects. *Jotoshiki*, a ritual to pray for the safety of a building, is less common than the popular groundbreaking *jichin-sai*, but it is still very much alive.

Jotoshiki takes place after the skeletal structure of a building has been completed. The ceremony involves raising the uppermost, and final, piece of the framework, and is usually attended by all members of the construction crew as well as representatives of the architects and client. At times a huge affair, it becomes a friendly opportunity to mingle with many who work behind the scenes.

The larger the project, the grander the occasion. Celebratory red-and-white banners, curtains or tents are erected, every ritual is highly organized, and loudspeakers are even set up to ensure everyone can appreciate speeches, announcements and blessings.

Parties of construction workers, architects and clients don safety helmets to pose for commemorative group photos. Identified by their work uniforms, sometimes even wearing traditional festival *happi* coats, each group's members are recognized for their contribution to the project.

Though *jotoshiki* rituals vary from region to region in Japan, there is often an opportunity for some participants to make their mark before the final structural beam is installed in front of its audience.

For the Ginza Place project, Klein Dytham architecture (KDa) members were invited, along with construction engineers, to sign the building's final beam before it was hoisted in place by a ceremonial red-and-white braided rope. As a final touch, the beam was installed with gleaming gold-plated bolts. Such details may never be seen by the public, but they lie within buildings for posterity like secret commemorative plaques.

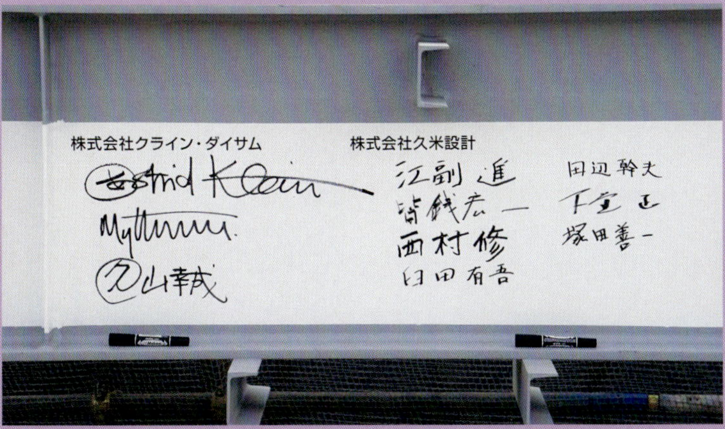
株式会社クライン・ダイサム
株式会社久米設計

祝 上棟
銀座5丁目再開発計画新築工事

祝 上棟
銀座5丁目再開発計画新築工事

祝 上棟
銀座5丁目再開発計画新築工事

"Revered artisans and meticulous attention to detail"

CARTIER SHINSAIBASHI BOUTIQUE

Osaka, Japan // Shop façade // 1,167 m²
Cartier // 2021

Cartier, located on a prominent corner of Shinsaibashi, a high-end shopping district of Osaka, shares an intersection with the metallic and glassy exteriors of Apple, Nike and Burberry. By contrast, its 3D wooden façade, designed by KDa, wraps the corner of the building, bringing an intimacy and warmth to the commercial area.

To create an environmentally conscious structure that reflects Cartier's involvement in responsible jewelry, KDa looked to renewable and recycled sources, as well as local artisanship. Hinoki (Japanese cypress) from Gifu Prefecture and Kyoto was chosen for its warm tones and historical background, and recycled aluminum was used in the structural framework.

Craftsmanship became a key focus of the design, a reflection of Cartier's revered artisans and meticulous attention to detail, paralleled with Japan's renowned traditional crafts.

The geometric pattern of gently protruding interlocking diamonds takes inspiration from both classic Cartier jewelry and Japanese traditional hinoki *masu* (sake boxes).

Twelve different hinoki units were designed to compose the main façade, its corners, skirting, and arched window details. In total, more than 2,500 units were used, each individually handcrafted and finished by Kyoto master carpenters using time-honored joinery techniques.

With the shop situated at the base of an existing building, a double-height entrance arch and side windows have been left open to draw attention to the two floors of the store. With only a 200-millimeter zone to work with between the existing building and the boundary line, the challenge was affixing the façade to the existing structure. For this, an aluminum frame was constructed to support the hinoki units as panels, which were lowered into place from above.

Cartier

Cartier

A material used for temples, shrines and castles, as well as for Japanese baths and tableware, hinoki is naturally stable and weather resistant. For the Cartier façade, its natural grain and tone are further protected with a waterproof and UV-resistant clear lacquer.

In the morning, its northeast-facing side is lit up by sunlight, enhancing the wood's characteristic beauty. Osaka, though, is as much alive in the evening as it is during shopping hours. To keep the façade striking at night, LED lights behind each unit illuminate the structure. Diffused by the box-like diamond of each section, the effect increases the three-dimensionality of the façade, and gives it an inviting, warm glow.

Cartier
Cartier

Cartier

"Welcome back to the books"

DAIKANYAMA T-SITE

Tokyo, Japan // Retail, apartment // 5,606 m²
Tsutaya, Culture Convenience Club // 2011

KDa's Daikanyama T-SITE is a campus-like complex for Tsutaya, a giant in Japan's book, music and movie retail market. Located in Daikanyama, an upmarket but relaxed low-rise Tokyo shopping district, it stands alongside a series of buildings designed by Pritzker Prize-winning architect Fumihiko Maki.

Drawing on all KDa's design skills—architecture, interior, furniture, and product display—the project's ambition was to define a new vision for the future of retailing. Tsutaya's usual product range is enhanced by a series of boutique spaces carrying carefully curated merchandise. This selection of goods is intended not to be exhaustive but stimulating: sections include art, architecture, cooking, cars, design, history, and literature. Each section is managed by a concierge who, much like the store's target clientele, possesses expert knowledge of the subject area. They keep customers informed about new book arrivals, and upcoming events and exhibitions in the store. T-SITE truly pioneered the concept of "social retail", transforming the space into a dynamic community hub where commerce meets curated experiences and meaningful interactions.

Cunningly solving a number of planning issues, including retention of the beautiful trees standing on the site, the complex was set back from the street and split into three pavilions. This arrangement of two- and three-story buildings creates relaxed walkways between them. Two bridges clad in polished stainless-steel battens connect the pavilions, reflecting the surroundings and creating gateways for visitors. In the design of the pavilion exteriors, KDa's characteristic wit emerges in subtle ways—the perforated screens of the façade are formed from the Ts of the Tsutaya logo, and much larger T-shapes are disguised in the building plans and elevations. The Ts are no mere graphic play, but provide fully 3D organizing principles, guiding how the plan is laid out and defining the arrangement of the structural system.

蔦屋書店
TSUTAYA BOOKS

蔦屋書店
TSUTAYA BOOKS

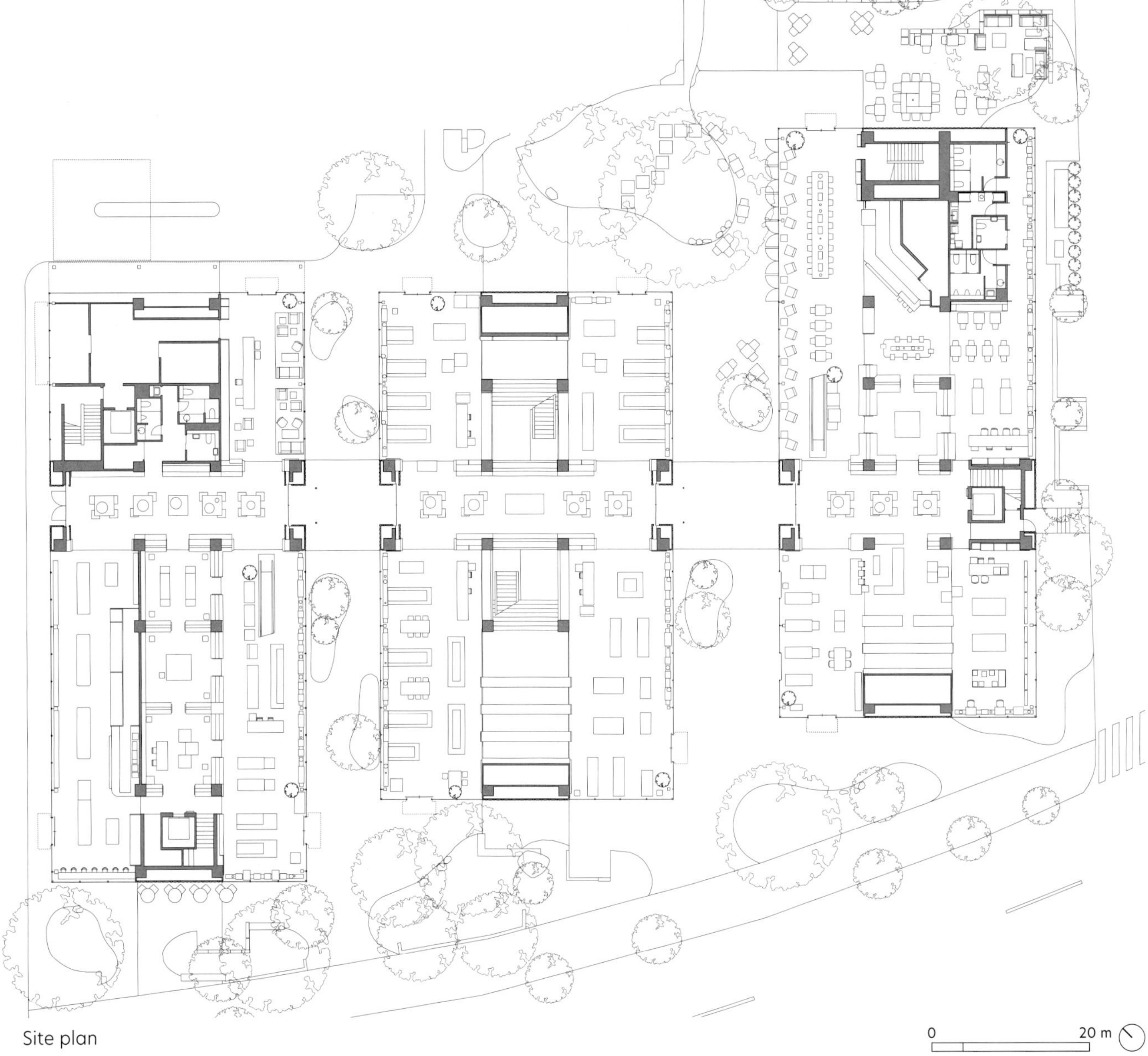

Site plan

The pavilions contain retail space on the lower floors with accommodation above. KDa didn't want a slick "department store" feel, and so selected materials such as aged timber flooring to create a relaxed space—part university library, part warehouse. The three pavilions are linked by an organizational spine called the "magazine street", which passes through interiors and exteriors, linking the three buildings. To reinforce its presence, the magazine street's shelving, flooring and slatted ceiling are all timber, even where it runs outside under the bridge. Elsewhere, a stone floor creates continuity between interiors and exteriors, while an open ceiling gives a warehouse feel. Large lanterns hang down to subtly mask the buildings' inner workings, and signage designed by Kenya Hara was printed on perforated metal to create more openness and visibility.

3
2F MUSIC
1F BOOKS
FOOD+COOKING
TRAVEL
STATIONERY

140028
AXIS
ARTnews
craft arts
FIGARO

ワールドミュージック
ワールドミュージック
新作
販売
THIS IS JAZZ
COFFEE BREAK CHRISTMAS
COFFEE BREAK JAZZ
SINATRA
JAZZ GIANTS 1961-2002
BLUE NOTE RECORDS

Within this organizational and material framework, each of the boutique spaces has its own character: the shelving in the literature section is tightly packed to evoke Tokyo's atmospheric Jimbocho secondhand-book district, while overhead shelves are used to make other spaces feel more intimate. Facilities include a café, an upscale convenience store, and the Anjin Lounge. Located in the center of the complex, this lounge includes a bar, a performance space, and a collection of artworks and rare books for sale that visitors can enjoy as they eat, drink, read, chat, or relax. Visitors to the lounge can also browse an amazing world magazine archive that includes beautifully bound collections of classics such as *Domus*, *Esquire* and *Abitare*—an entire class of fashion students was spotted pouring over back issues of *Vogue*.

Despite its design innovations, this was not a big-budget project—it was low cost and produced quickly. The whole project was completed in 20 months, with construction taking just 11 months despite disruptions caused by the Tohoku earthquake and tsunami. KDa was awarded the project through an invited competition. Its scheme triumphed over those of many of Japan's highest-profile architectural firms by tackling both explicit branding issues and architectural subtleties in every aspect of the building. Merging the digital and analog worlds, and providing for both sophisticated tastes and simple curiosity, KDa's design has created a new retail paradigm to emerge.

PERSPECTIVES ON GALBRAITH
INTERNATIONAL DEBT

"Ivy league"

SHONAN T-SITE

Fujisawa, Japan // Commercial complex // 7,406 m²
Tsutaya, Culture Convenience Club // 2014

Taking on many of the ideas that were developed for Daikanyama T-SITE in Tokyo, this is KDa's second T-SITE bookstore project for Tsutaya, Japan's leading media and retail company.

The building is located just 2 kilometers from the famous Shonan coast. The area's strong surf vibe was a key influence on making this project relaxed, informal and approachable, but the former factory site was very different from the first T-SITE project in the leafy area of Daikanyama.

By creating a series of gateways or portals that were shifted along a central axis, it was possible to create pocket parks and natural entrances. The portals were shifted vertically as well as horizontally to allow light into the central areas of the building and help modulate the architecture of the building.

Tsutaya, the name of the company, is written in two kanji characters: *tsuta* and *ya*. *Tsuta* means ivy and *ya* means house, which inspired the ivy pattern on the façade. This was not only important to soften the project with leaves, but also made up for the lack of greenery by idea association.

SHONAN T-SI

"A place for books, kids, and picnics by the lake"

KASHIWANOHA T-SITE

Chiba, Japan // Commercial complex // 5,953 m²
Tsutaya, Culture Convenience Club // 2017

Kashiwanoha T-SITE is a key element of Kashiwanoha Campus, one of Japan's pioneering smart cities. Designed to balance the urban scale with human-centered spaces, the complex aims to create a comfortable "third place" for both residents and visitors from surrounding areas—a vibrant hub where people can meet, interact and build a sense of community.

Inspired by the successful designs of Daikanyama T-SITE and Shonan T-SITE, Kashiwanoha T-SITE integrates outdoor and indoor spaces harmoniously with its environment. With the complex originally located next to a fenced-off balancing lake, KDa spearheaded the area's transformation into a publicly accessible waterfront, now featuring a boardwalk and terraces that invite the community to engage with the space. This integration of nature and architecture creates a place where people can experience the changing beauty of the landscape across different times of the day and throughout the seasons.

The complex itself consists of five interconnected buildings, unified by a 110-meter-long "magazine street". This central walkway seamlessly connects a range of specialty shops on both sides, creating a natural flow between books, magazines, and lifestyle goods, and offering a cohesive cultural and retail experience. The small, intimate spaces formed by the architecture give the complex a welcoming, home-like atmosphere.

The upper floor of Kashiwanoha T-SITE is designed with families in mind, featuring children's books, after-school programs and workshop facilities. This thoughtful design fosters a sense of discovery and engagement, particularly for young families. Overall, the complex serves not only as a retail destination but as a dynamic cultural hub, enhancing the lifestyle of Kashiwanoha residents and creating an inviting space for visitors to enjoy.

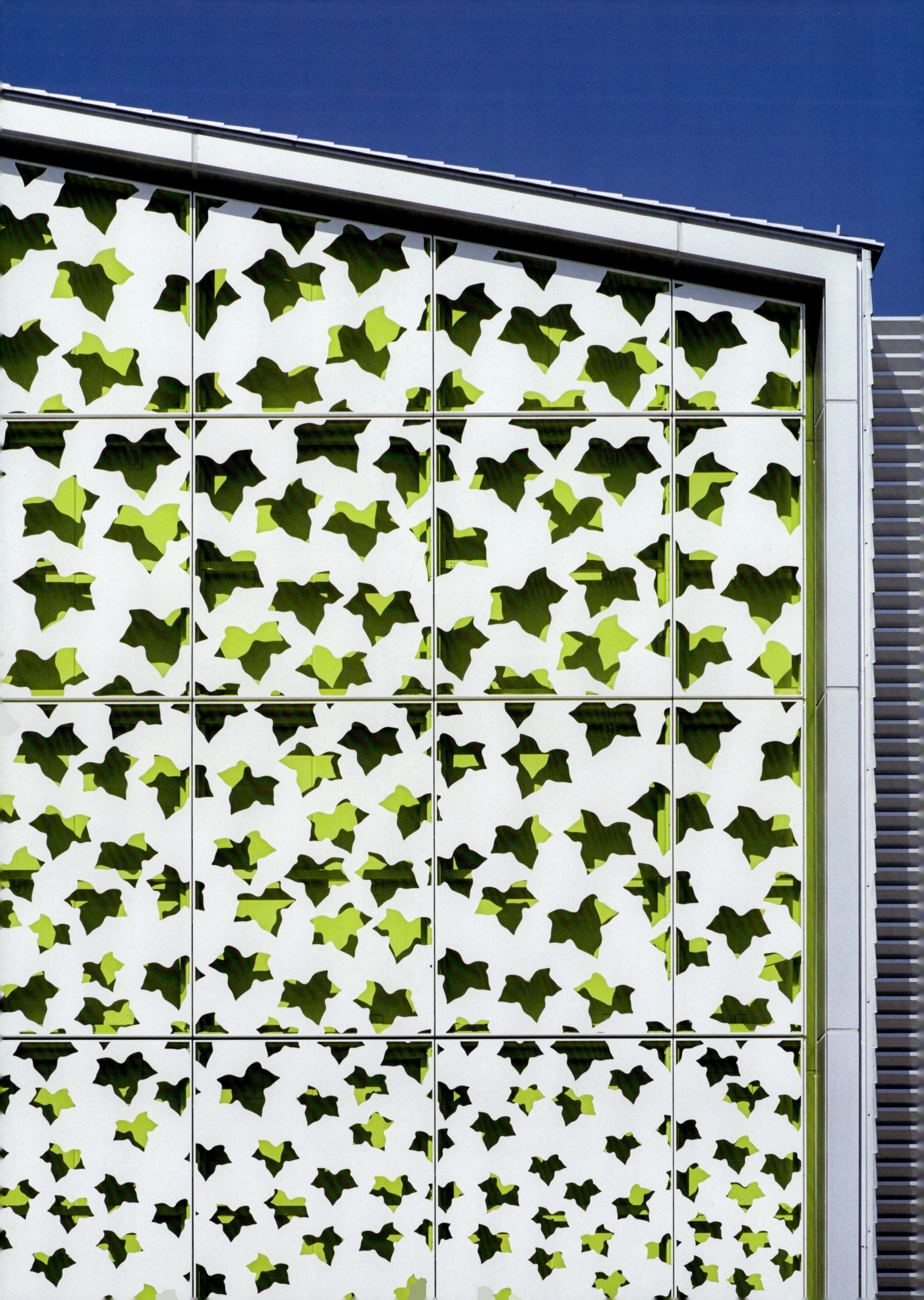

KASHIWANOHA T-SITE

"A neighborhood lobby"

NAKAMEGURO TSUTAYA BOOKS

Tokyo, Japan // Bookstore, café // 439 m²
Tsutaya, Culture Convenience Club // 2016

Situated beneath the elevated train tracks of Tokyo's Nakameguro Station, Nakameguro Tsutaya Books is an unconventional iteration of a bookstore. Selling a variety of magazines and gifts, it has a café, and it's the first structure travelers see as they exit the station—a welcoming hub of activity that lights up its unusual location like a lantern.

Following the same visual language of Daikanyama T-SITE, Nakameguro Tsutaya Books uses simpler, more industrial materials inspired by its surroundings.

A passage splits the store into two sections, creating an off-street, enclosed but inviting intimacy. Wrapped around the top third of the structure's glass façade, a belt of white sheet metal featuring a cut-out pattern of tessellating T-shapes is backlit to emit a warm, comforting glow. Instead of window displays, comfy red sofas face out to the pavement, allowing visitors to view the streets as they browse through magazines or relax with a coffee.

The seating and shelving disguise a challenging aspect of Nakameguro Tsutaya Books—its layout of numerous hefty concrete columns supporting the railroad above. To transform these into functional features, contrasting lightweight furniture was used, their slender frameworks designed to be easily removed for routine pillar inspections. Some columns become the backrests of sofas, others are lined with racks and shelves for magazines and stylish selections of lifestyle goods. The spaces between create cozy reading nooks, while long communal tables in the café area offer more areas to leisurely peruse publications.

A popular and convenient rendezvous spot, magazine outlet, boutique, and relaxed space to take a break before catching the train home, Nakameguro Tsutaya Books serves as a lobby to the Tokyo neighborhood.

蔦屋書店
STAFF ONLY

中目黒
Naka-meguro
なかめぐろ
代官山
WOVE clinic
美容皮膚科
皮膚科
シミ・肝斑治療センター併設
ウォブクリニック中目黒
0120-411-281
中目黒駅より徒歩3分
JIYUGAOKA CLINIC
自由が丘クリニック
Tel 03-5701-2500
ここから
夜間押ボタン式
蔦屋書店
STARBUCKS

住みかえに、
安心と安全を。
住友不動産販売
中目黒営業センター
0120-112-474
おいしいピュアウォーター
alpina
蔦屋書店
TSUTAYA BOOKS
STARBUCKS

"Like a lantern lighting the way in a forest"

COMMONGROUNDS

Karuizawa, Japan // Bookstore, café, coworking space // 495 m²
Tsutaya, Culture Convenience Club // 2023

Karuizawa Commongrounds lies in one of Japan's oldest resort towns, nestled between the mountains of Nagano at the foot of Mount Asama. The project is designed as a community hub for Karuizawa residents. It comprises a main bookstore surrounded by five small buildings hosting local businesses, including a delicatessen, a wine store, a soba restaurant, and a preschool. The location, a historically popular summer retreat for the Imperial family, surrounds the complex with views of lush woodland and majestic distant peaks.

The bookstore is the heart of the complex. An extension wraps around the lower half of the original building, its sheet-steel roof hugging the structure like a twirling skirt. The roof's flowing arches, echoed by its soft, inward-curving eaves, evoke the highland terrain of the location as they extend beyond the extension's glass walls to shelter a surrounding terrace. To the south, the terrace doubles as a long bench, where a continuous wooden counter allows visitors to sit and look out on a peaceful mini meadow. By nightfall, the glass walls and second-floor windows emit a welcoming glow, like a lantern lighting the way in a forest.

Inside, simple plywood furnishings match a ceiling of exposed wooden beams. Shelves filled with books wrap around the original structure, the middle of which is left open as a double-height space stretching through to the second floor.

When Karuizawa Commongrounds' construction began, the walls of the Showa-era building were completely dismantled, leaving only wooden interior beams and its staircase. From the high ceiling, long pendant lamps hang through the opening to float over the first floor, and a counter stretches along the north-facing windows for visitors to read or work. The flanking coworking areas provide cozy and quieter spaces. Both are carpeted and divided by bookshelves into individual booths.

An economical and environmentally conscious project, the structure's steel supports, roof panels and other materials are manufactured locally, and the pitched roof features solar panels. Outside, the meadow and woodland are cultivated using permaculture principles, while a small vegetable farm allows children to explore nature.

"A never-ending bookstore"

UMEDA TSUTAYA BOOKS

Osaka, Japan // Retail // 4,097 m²
Tsutaya, Culture Convenience Club // 2015

An immense book, magazine, and lifestyle store, Umeda Tsutaya Books is a complete transformation of the entire ninth floor of LUCUA, a department store directly connected to Osaka Station.

Sitting between LUCUA's restaurant and fashion floors, its expansive space is divided by Magazine Street, a central loop of shelving, lined inside and out with publications from around the world. Like a racetrack, but one to be perused by the literary-minded, a pedestrian lane circles the shelving, with pit stops of tables stacked with more books and magazines. An outer loop offers simple, cushioned seating to encourage browsing, separated by columns wrapped in more shelves of books and collections of contemporary lifestyle goods.

The radial plan is built in deep, warm wood tones, complemented by a real tree that stretches upwards through the double-height central space to branch over the relaxing heart of Magazine Street: its Garden Lounge of comfy seating, tables and greenery. Alongside the lounge, escalators take visitors to other floors, and a café serves light refreshments.

Umeda Tsutaya Books is more than a simple bookstore. Outside its unique Magazine Street, a ring of establishments offer lifestyle services, including beauty goods, a hair salon, an Apple service center, watch repairs, wedding services, and other cafés. Its location, directly linked to Osaka Station, provides commuters and visitors with a peaceful but social haven to take a break from the hubbub of city life.

蔦屋書店
TSUTAYA BOOKS

Helvetica
forever
ゴッホ

日本文学
JAPANESE LITERATURE | 日本文学

"Color is free ... use it"

TOGGLE HOTEL SUIDOBASHI

Tokyo, Japan // Hotel // 3,219 m²
Saison Realty // 2020

Toggle Hotel is truly an urban hotel, located in the heart of Tokyo. The triangular site is bound by the Metropolitan Expressway flying over an extension of the historic Imperial moat on one side, while the Chuo Line, the main railway line that crosses Tokyo, runs past on the opposite side.

The building was designed to be a new iconic landmark to reflect Tokyo's energy and vitality. So often one passes buildings on a train or in a car and they seem nondescript, so it was important for Toggle Hotel to stand out and advertise itself—something to be recognized and help locate you in Tokyo's urban jungle.

Responding to the gray monochrome urban setting, the architecture and interior of Toggle Hotel are all about movement and color. The architecture emphasizes the horizontal movement of the cars and trains, with continuous window bands that trace the dynamism of the urban infrastructure and express speed. The fresh yellow and concrete gray pattern was inspired by the graphic patterns on the expressway. Although the design and color of the building were approved by the city council almost 2 years before completion, KDa was on point—the exact gray and yellow were the 2021 Pantone Colors of the year!

The reception lobby is on the top floor of the building, which also acts as the café and main social hub of the hotel. Glazed on three sides, generous green terraces give great views of the city and the 50,000-seat Tokyo Dome, which is located nearby. Fans attending concerts and events are some of the guests at this hotel.

TOYOTA

Section

The hotel is positioned as a stylish yet economical place to stay in Tokyo. Around 60 percent of the rooms have loft-type beds, which allow three people to stay in one room. Each floor of the hotel has a different color combination, which is reflected in the ten types of rooms as well. Choose your favorite color combination! KDa worked with a graphic design team, artless, which developed the logo, graphics, and branding for the hotel. The two-color combination is even reflected in the soft furnishings for the room.

The hotel gets its name, Toggle, from the notion that you can be "on" or "off" at the hotel. On for work or off for leisure; equally, off for work and on for leisure. Whether you are staying at the hotel for business, leisure, or train spotting, each stay is guaranteed to be colorful, different, and fun!

"Pixel perfect"

THE TOMAMU TOWERS

Hokkaido, Japan // Hotel façade // 22,000 m² (Façade area)
Hoshino Resorts // 2008

Located in the forest-covered mountains of central Hokkaido, the alpine resort town of Tomamu is an outdoor recreation paradise. Standing in this beautiful landscape are the forty-story hotel towers of the Alpha Resort, which has a mixed architectural heritage—the complex includes Tadao Ando's famous Chapel on the Water, designed as a wedding chapel, and two hotel towers built during the economic boom of the late 1980s. The towers stand 121 meters tall—so high that in the winter the cloud layer is often lower than the top of the towers. In 2006 the two aging towers needed recladding, so the resort's owners asked KDa to develop a color scheme to reduce their prominence.

Wanting to reduce the impact of the towers within this beautiful landscape, KDa decided to use camouflage, but the difficulty was that the natural environment surrounding the resort changes constantly with the seasons. KDa's solution was to camouflage one tower to suit winter conditions and the other to suit summer: one tower fades from black to white, and the other from green to white.

While KDa wanted to dissolve the building's mass, they didn't want invisibility and so inserted a few red panels to liven things up. Their inspiration was the cheerful red baubles on a Christmas tree—rather than being around for just one day a year, the red panels create smiles year-round.

The extraordinary size of the buildings and the boldness of the color schemes create a surreal scene usually only possible in computer renderings!

"Eleven stories imagined as a layered wedding cake"

Q PLAZA HARAJUKU

Tokyo, Japan // Commercial complex // 8,105 m²
Tokyu Land // 2015

Q Plaza Harajuku is located on Meiji Dori between the bustling center of Shibuya and the lush green oasis of Meiji Shrine and leafy shopping area of Omotesando.

The building site was very deep, but only has a narrow frontage onto the street. Taking advantage of new planning regulations in the area, the building rises to eleven stories adjacent to the road, and its form is dictated by creating the maximum floor area possible. The back of the building is low-rise and was developed as a series of lush green terraces allowing for extended views onto the woods of a shrine.

Although the building is intended for mixed use, its main purpose is for wedding ceremonies and it contains a large chapel on the terrace's lower floors, so the rest of the eleven stories are imagined as a layered wedding cake, with each floor stacked on the next. The fin façade was developed to bring color, movement and filtered transparency to the building. When approached along Meiji Dori toward leafy Omotesando, the building's fins are green. On the other hand, for those walking toward lively Shibuya, the fins are bright pink. At night the orange fins softly glow like candles.

Nail Labo

"Tokyo electro-retro meets Ginza glitz"

UNIQLO GINZA

Tokyo, Japan // Retail // 5,000 m²
Uniqlo // 2005

Uniqlo has built its brand by providing basic clothing at reasonable prices. Similarly, KDa's approach to Uniqlo Ginza was to aim for simple and basic. If façades in 2005 were screens, the Uniqlo façade is a pixilated "electro-retro" version. It is made of a matrix of 1,000 illuminated cells, whose luminosity can be individually controlled to produce chunky Tetris-style patterns.

A mirror-finish stainless-steel grid placed over this screen has the effect of breaking up and blurring its sharp edges. The square Uniqlo logo shines through it, lit up with a bright LED array: luxury at low-res.

For the Ginza store, Uniqlo needed a warmer, more sophisticated interior than the casual environments it is known for. Each floor is distinguished by a different color displaying products for distinct target markets, from gallery white on the entry level for fresh promotions and campaigns, through magnolia and cinnamon, to deep chocolate on the menswear floor.

KDa also devised a flexible, modular display and shelving system, comprising a "pergola" element and stackable low tables. These bring a sense of domestic scale and comfort to the Ginza glitz.

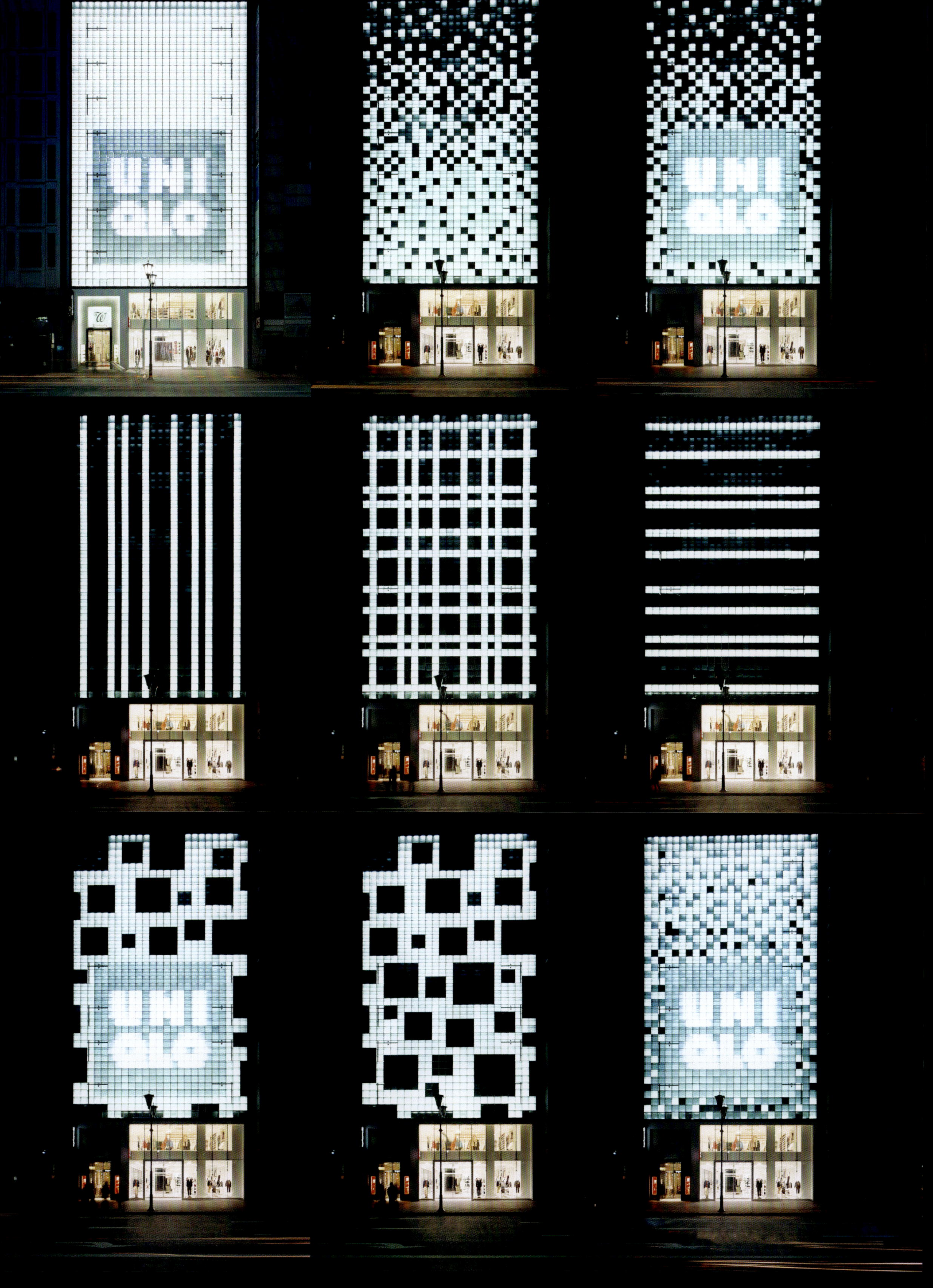
UNI
QLO

"Echoes the dynamic and blurred swoosh of the Shinkansen trains"

ATAMI STATION BUILDING

Atami, Japan // Railway station commercial complex // 7,677 m²
East Japan Railway Company // 2016

Completed in 2016, Atami Station stands at the heart of one of Japan's oldest seaside resorts along the coast of Shizuoka Prefecture. Just 45 minutes from Tokyo by bullet train, its 140-meter-long, four-story station building stretches ahead of Japan Railway's East, Central and Tokaido Shinkansen lines, and houses a busy shopping mall of more than 30 stores.

Inspired by Atami's coastal views, a façade of elongated concrete panels forms a fluctuating ombré of blues to whites that soften the building's steel block-like structure. Deep azures gradually ascend to powder blues, linking the colors of the sea to the clouds in the sky. Extended windows, divided into grids of rectangles like shoji screens of picturesque Japanese hot-spring hotels, create a visual flow between exterior and interior.

Non-uniformity brings movement to the design. Façade panels are flat or ridged, some shiny, others matte. Their staggered colors surround asymmetrically placed windows like horizontal speed lines. From a distance, the entire station—with its shimmering glass and dashes of blue and white—echoes the dynamic and blurred swoosh of the Shinkansen trains that race by it every day.

"Nothing like an engine block aesthetic"

BMW GROUP TOKYO BAY

Tokyo, Japan // Showroom // 7,176 m²
BMW Tokyo Group // 2016

Occupying an entire block of Tokyo's futuristic waterfront Odaiba district, the flagship showroom offers a complete brand experience for both car enthusiasts and casual visitors. Opened in 2016 to celebrate BMW's 100th anniversary, its grounds include a BMW showroom, a MINI showroom, a café, an auditorium, a garage, and a track where visitors can test-drive over ninety cars.

A silvery structure sits at the heart of the complex, its curving perforated canopy casting dramatic shadows over the entrance to the café and auditorium. The canopy's circular design forms a 3D ceiling of brightly lit cells.

The BMW showroom features over more than twenty parked in a street that parallels a strip of consulting booths and a spacious bar, while the vehicles in the compact MINI showroom are geometrically laid out around a meeting hub of intersecting rectangular frames. By design, the strikingly different appearance of BMW Group Tokyo Bay's central zone unites the two showrooms, each informed by corporate identity aesthetics and architectural guidelines.

"Why can't a skyscraper be fun?"

SUPER MODEL

Tokyo, Japan // Exhibition // 42 floors
Tokyo Design Week // 2012

Nowadays a multitude of software and advanced technologies allow the design of tall buildings in all sorts of shapes and forms without limits. But the struggle to design yet another elegant and iconic skyscraper becomes ever harder. KDa often asks, "What would we do were we asked to design such a skyscraper?" There seems to be no easy answer.

Architecture at this scale is a very serious matter: it is an enormous financial investment, it is a structural challenge, and it is a maze of logistics in terms of infrastructure and management. Ideally it has to be ecological and sustainable. And last but not least, it will be a landmark in the city for years to come.

But do all these very valid reasons justify that there should be no fun in architecture? Is it all right to alienate the citizens with yet another imposing skyscraper? Or could there be room for an identifiable building shape that puts a smile on people's faces? Why can't a skyscraper be fun?

KitKat

The journey of the KitKat, from a British imported chocolate bar to a popular fixture of Japanese culture, is a sweet story of inspiring design.

KDa arrived in Japan around the same time Nestlé opened its first Japanese KitKat factory in 1989. The evolution of KitKat flavors and packaging is a joyful primer of Japan's ingenuity and design idiosyncrasies—the characteristics of a creative community that has kept KDa in Tokyo.

The KitKat's piecemeal development over three decades essentially expresses a work ethic of constant invention and reinvention, a willingness to micro-experiment and refine, uncompromising attention to detail, and a subtle sense of playfulness. It's a unique perspective of design and marketing that has been so successful, it transformed a British confectionery into a popular souvenir of Japan.

There is so much to unwrap here. The hundreds of KitKat flavors—from simple strawberry or red apple to eyebrow-raising soy sauce and wasabi—reflect an unfettered enthusiasm to embrace new originality. Limited-edition packaging and countless regional and seasonal specialties showcase Nestlé Japan's creative localisation and curation, combined with a mastery of innovative graphic design.

No stone is left unturned. Campaigns respect culture by paying homage to the forty-seven prefectures of Japan with whimsical local editions. Collaborations run the gamut, from ingredients honed by sake makers and high-end chefs to package designs inspired by public transport and the post office. Each time there's a new release, it's a different flavor, a new design or a redesign. Such diversity can only be born from lateral thinking and an open-minded attitude toward unconventionality.

In Japan, architecture thrives on this unparalleled eagerness to embrace and experiment with new ideas. Like a savory KitKat in the chocolate business, there's the freedom to try things that architects elsewhere normally couldn't or wouldn't consider—unconventional materials, structurally complex forms, unusual motifs.

We also find façades and interiors to be great "packaging" of buildings. As an integral part of aesthetics, façades and interiors take architecture beyond a structure's function. Like huge manifestations of graphic design, they are calling cards to engage and resonate with an audience visually and, most importantly, emotionally. It's what brings a smile to visitors and keeps them returning—just like the fans and followers of KitKat's never-ending series of new flavors and designs.

1枚あたり
97 kcal
Nestlé
KitKat
きなこおはぎ味
〈きな粉香料・小豆香料使用〉
〈もち米パフ0.7%使用〉 写真はイメージです

1枚あたり
114 kcal
Nestlé
KitKat
キットカット サクラサク
大学いも味
期間限定
写真はイメージです

Nestlé
KitKat
冷やして美味しい
大納言
あずき
〈あずき香料使用〉

Nestlé
KitKat
UNIVERSAL STUDIOS JAPAN
5 Years
ユニバーサル・スタジオ・ジャパン™
5周年記念限定商品
きっと願いかなう
星に願いを

Nestlé
KitKat
京都
宇治抹茶
京都限定
写真はイメージです

1枚あたり
100 kcal
Nestlé
KitKat
ジンジャーエール味
Ginger Ale
写真はイメージです
レモンパウダー0.3%使用
ジンジャーエール香料使用

1枚あたり
100 kcal
クックパッド
おすすめ商品
Nestlé
KitKat
アップルビネガー
Apple Vinegar
写真はイメージです
りんご酢パウダー1.4%使用
りんご香料使用

北海道
小豆
期間限定
Nestlé
KitKat
写真はイメージです
〈小豆香料使用〉

甲信越地区
限定販売
Nestlé
KitKat
巨峰
Kyoho
Grape
写真はイメージです

"The new façade rises to the occasion"

OLIVE LOUNGE SHIBUYA

Tokyo, Japan // Coworking space, bank, café // 1,765 m²
Sumitomo Mitsui Banking + Tsutaya, Culture Convenience Club // 2004

Olive Lounge Shibuya's façade is visually striking. SMBC's familiar logo is re-imagined into walls of glossy glass panels, the smooth curves of the expanded glass elements creating captivating reflections and subtle visual distortions. Narrow spaces between the bank's original and new glass façade are transformed into plant-filled atriums, bringing a touch of nature to the urban landscape.

An olive tree, a symbol of peace and growth, welcomes visitors to the first floor. A fusion of modern banking and lifestyle, the first floor seamlessly combines a lively Starbucks café corner with SMBC's banking services. ATM booths are tucked away at the back alongside an open-plan consulting area that doubles as extra café seating after 3 pm. The contour of curved upholstered bench seating outlines a casual meeting area.

Open to anyone (for a fee), the second-floor Share Lounge features a drinks counter, cozy work booths, curved study tables, window-seating and two circular glass-walled meeting rooms. A lowered wood ceiling provides more intimacy in a corner section that can be closed off to become an event space. For ultimate focus, an original SMBC bank vault is repurposed into an enclosed area of seven work booths, its chunky, solid-steel safe door and mammoth bar locks becoming a whimsical design focus of the Share Lounge.

Square columns of the building's original structure are clad in wood and converted into high counter tables. Both the first floor and Share Lounge feature the gentle arches of Karimoku chairs and tables. Meeting rooms are all given the increased comfort of Fumie Shibata's ergonomic Vertebra chairs designed for Itoki Furniture.

In the basement of Olive Lounge Shibuya, KDa's doradora modular furniture, in a luxurious, forest-green velvet, forms a circular casual meeting spot to welcome guests ahead of private meeting rooms wrapped in partially frosted glass. Another original vault is left virtually intact as a large meeting room, its hundreds of shiny safe deposit boxes lining the walls for a retro-futuristic aesthetic that, again, pays homage to the prestigious nature of past bank buildings.

olive
LOUNGE
SMBC

SHARE LOUNGE
Olive
LOUNGE
三井住友銀行

STARBUCKS
STARBUCKS
Olive
LOUNGE

SEIBU
Olive
SHARE LOUNGE
LOUNGE
SMBC

井ノ頭通り入口
Inokashiradori St.
スクランブル交差点
Olive
LOUNGE
終日
20-7

"Why doesn't every city have an Open House?"

OPEN HOUSE, CENTRAL EMBASSY

Bangkok, Thailand // Bookstore, restaurants, cafés, coworking // 4,600 m²
Central Group // 2017

Open House is located in the Central Embassy complex 50 meters above Bangkok. Within this vast 4,600-square-meter double-height interior, a village of spaces has been created—restaurants, lounges, bars, galleries, stores, pop-ups, libraries, and workspaces—that all seamlessly fit together.

Today's mega cities are all about working, shopping, eating or transitioning between spaces. There is nowhere to pause, take a breath, sit, or simply get back in control of your senses, especially in the stifling heat of Bangkok. Open House is seen very much as the antidote to this. It is an oasis, a getaway, a place where one can feel at home.

The brief required around fourteen restaurants and bars, a bookstore, a coworking space, a kids' space, and various communal areas. With so many components and functions, it was clear that navigation was the key. How could an aircraft-hanger-like space be converted into a seamlessly connected village?

By developing a series of towers for each of the restaurants, KDa could make the restaurants visible from a distance. The towers are clad in different timber fretwork patterns; the variety in these patterns serves to change the way light passes through the towers as one moves through the room. In daylight, the towers seem more solid, while at night they dissolve, creating interesting layering effects and moiré patterns. Mirrored panels on the ceiling around the towers make them appear to extend beyond the space and also break down the immensity of the ceiling.

The bookstore element, rather than being a large square box, is linear and weaves its way through the space, a path with areas where visitors can pause and read. A tall book tower anchors the bookstore at one end, and a large double-height library wall wraps around at the other end of the space. The bookstore seamlessly integrates into the bar and restaurant spaces and allows people to browse freely. In a world dominated by online book sales, highly curated bookstores like this, which focus on Asian art and culture, are becoming increasingly important and popular.

by MUGENDAI

Open House includes a coworking space behind the book wall, and provides a quieter, more secluded space for working, plus a suite of meeting rooms.

The Central Embassy complex is in a leafy area of Bangkok, overlooking the British Embassy complex on one side and treetops on the other. To bring a green canopy inside, and reduce the impact of the extensive white ceiling, 9,600 leaves were hand painted on the ceiling, creating an amazing artwork, an iconic and memorable element of the environment.

Activating the space with talks, book signings and other events is key to keeping the space alive and a vital part of the city. "The steps" seating allows for this, while also providing seating when it is not being used for events, and the kids' play zone is abuzz with noise and fun. Open House truly is for everyone.

Over the last few years Bangkok has become a sophisticated world-class retail and food destination. With the city changing so quickly, the challenge was how to design something that would always be a part of the moment and a familiar retreat—a true Open House.

Since its opening the space has been a huge success, it is used by locals and tourists alike. The most common question? "Why doesn't every city have an Open House?"

ART TOWER

muteki
by MUGENDAI

THE Raw Bar
Oyster·Lobster·Moules
MEAT BAR

muteki
BONSAI
JAPANESE CHESTS
KODANSHA

WORKSHOP DESK
TASCHEN
FORMULA 1
KOREAN CULTURE
A Cultural History of Modern Korea

"Artists are angels and our job is to give them wings to fly"

FENDER FLAGSHIP TOKYO

Tokyo, Japan // Guitar store // 1,068 m²
Fender Music // 2023

Harajuku, Tokyo's vibrant street-style shopping destination, is the apt home of Fender's first flagship store of its nearly 80-year history of pioneering electric guitar design. An interior renovation of the iconic glass-walled Ice Cubes building, the store opens up four floors to offer a chic and unprecedented guitar-shopping environment. As a hub of all things Fender, it's an immersive retail experience—a destination of discovery that includes personalized customer services, bespoke guitars, gallery exhibits, an event space, a café, and opportunities to try instruments and equipment.

Aware that guitar stores can be intimidating, Fender requested a design that emphasized the artisanship and heritage of its guitars to create a sophisticated retail experience that would encourage leisurely browsing.

The first floor sets the stage, with benches and display units in light warm woods that mirror the smooth curves of Fender guitars to create winding lines of arcs that guide visitors into the airy space. Above, light fixtures parallel and reinforce these waved contours. Large graphic walls, flanked by display shelves of guitars, tell the Fender story and draw the eye to the newest and most popular products.

Instruments are treated like luxury designer goods, taken down and shown to shoppers on pick-shaped tables. At the rear, an alcove is home to the brand's latest venture, F IS FOR FENDER, a capsule collection of designer streetwear. Behind a central service counter, an embroidered winged-guitar illustration features Leo Fender's most inspiring quote, "Artists are angels and our job is to give them wings to fly."

Such angels are introduced at the building's spiral staircase, which is transformed into a hall-of-fame photo gallery, its walls hosting 150 images of illustrious Fender players. The steps lead customers upwards to more focused, intimate, and luxurious experiences—Fender's own stairway to heaven.

KEN STRATOCASTER®
EXPERIMENT #1
AMERICAN VINTAGE II

KEN STRATOCASTE
EXPERIMENT #1
GUESS

AMERICAN VINTAGE II
Fender

MADE IN JAPAN JUNIOR COLLECTION
FEATURES
Down-Scaled Body for Super Comfortable Playability
Reduced Body Weight with New Cavity Design
Short Scale Neck for Astounding Fret Feel

On the second floor, where the color palette switches to a soft gray, visitors are immediately met by an Artists Gallery that splits the shopping area into two sections. A changing exhibition of large-scale dramatic images of eminent musicians is paired with transparent display cases housing their guitars of choice. At the back, an LED video wall screens footage of the celebrities in action. To one side of the gallery is a Made in Japan space showcasing Japan-crafted classic and limited-edition Telecasters, Stratocasters, Jazzmasters, basses and more. On the other side is a Made in America counterpart. A soundproofed Amp Room at the back allows customers to try out and familiarize themselves with any Fender guitar and amp.

HARLEY DAVIDSON
90TH ANNIVERSARY
STRATOCASTER®
MONTEREY
STRATOCASTER®

MAYAN/AZTEC
EGYPTIAN ART
TELECASTER®
TELECASTER®

Fender

GUESS

As the pinnacle of Fender luxury, the third floor is one of rich charcoal grays and deep warm browns. Directly above the Artists Gallery lies the artisanal highlight of the Fender building—the Master Builders Gallery. Photographic portraits introduce the skilled craftspeople behind bespoke Fender guitars, alongside examples of their work. A multicolored shrine of 300 guitar-finish sample tiles lines the back wall, creating an alcove that illustrates an extraordinary diversity of color and textures. Two VIP rooms, each featuring glass display units of deluxe instruments, and a custom shop space provide comfy sofas for visitors to unwind and discuss bespoke options.

Beneath the Fender Flagship Tokyo's three shop floors lies a basement hive of social activity, a perfect foil to the third-floor premium experience. Here, plectrum-shaped benches and a plush rug add warm red accents to a casual event space that includes a corner café serving Fender's specialty coffee.

One final and dramatic detail adds to the Fender Flagship Tokyo experience: a huge central, vertical LED display on the exterior façade shows clips of celebrities with their guitars to passersby.

Fender
Fender
Fender

"Now that's what I call a mountain of books!"

THINK SPACE B2S

Bangkok, Thailand // Bookstore // 3,000 m²
Central Group, B2S // 2016

Think Space by B2S at Central Festival East Ville in Bangkok redefines the bookshop experience by seamlessly merging books and magazines with additional services.

Upon entering, visitors are immediately captivated by a striking mountain of books rising within the spacious three-story interior. This dramatic installation embodies the "book terrace" concept, where sloping mezzanine levels divide the floors. Staircases on both sides guide readers through towering bookshelves to the upper levels.

The third floor houses a café and coworking space, alongside a curated shop offering audio products adjacent to the CD and Vinyl Room. Nearby, a retail section presents a thoughtfully selected array of stationery and lifestyle items, chosen for their exceptional design quality. Think Space blends the immersive charm of a library with the dynamic energy of a modern bookshop, creating an inviting, intimate atmosphere.

Despite its many sections, the space remains interconnected through a network of pathways, ensuring seamless navigation. Merchandise is curated not by category but by thematic relationships, sparking serendipitous discoveries—art books sit beside painting supplies, while travel books share space with maps, cameras, and backpacks. This approach fosters creativity and inspiration, extending even to the spaces under the book terraces, which are reserved for creative talks and activities.

The combination of white and light brown bookshelves, a green carpet, real plants, abundant natural light streaming in from the skylight, and outdoor views makes reading a refreshing experience—akin to relaxing in an open-air café.

PLAY
THINK SPACE
FICTION
SMART
B2S
WIFE. MOM. BOSS.
BEST BOOKS FOR
#LADYBOSSES
BIG
TRAV

THINK SPACE

"I would rather stroll through a park than a shopping mall"

MOZO WONDER CITY

Nagoya, Japan // Shopping mall // 16,935 m²
Mitsubishi UBS Realty // 2009

Mozo Grove, a 220-meter-long renovated atrium, lies at the center of Mozo Wonder City, Japan's fifth-largest shopping complex, located on the outskirts of Nagoya. The project re-imagines the atrium, once a conventionally simple, open public space, into a lush interior park—a haven of greenery within the urban surroundings of Mozo Wonder City's more than 200 bustling stores.

At the heart of Mozo Grove, rows of tall, abstract trees, each made of slim steel pipes, draw visitors into and through the atrium. Rising from the first floor to 15 meters in height, their green, circular boughs branch out at different levels, forming a canopy of open rings that sweeps over passersby below.

The foundations of the trees are clad in wood panels to create platforms and benches where visitors can meet, pause among potted greenery, and leisurely window-shop from a distance. Hanging basket seats offer extra pockets of quietude on the first floor, while pathways of grassy green carpeting on the upper floors overlooking the atrium complete a verdant, landscaped vision of the shopping complex.

"A luxury goods emporium with the energy of a souk"

SELFRIDGES

London, England // Department store // 1,800 m²
Selfridges // 2007

KDa redesigned 1,800 square meters of luxury goods retail space on the ground floor of Selfridges & Co's famous Oxford Street store. Finding inspiration in the way stores fit neatly behind the existing architecture of London's Victorian shopping arcades, and in the notion of a *wunderkammer*—room-sized displays of interesting or exotic objects—KDa created the Wonder Room, a space that houses "a luxury goods emporium with the energy of a souk."

KDa devised an elegant wall of white-coated aluminum fins that runs around the perimeter of the room, with floating elegant, polished stainless-steel display cabinets between the fins. Rather than giving the individual brands complete freedom of expression, all the concessions are placed behind this façade, giving the Wonder Room a degree of uniformity and order. In the center of the Wonder Room are glass and high-gloss lacquer cabinets for displaying smaller items such as fine jewelry, watches, and luxury mobile phones.

Cartier

TIFFANY & Co.
Fashion Jewellery
Stationery
VERTU
VERTU
VERTU
VERTU

"Color like no other"

SONY STORE LOS ANGELES

Los Angeles, USA // Retail // 525 m²
Sony Global Retail // 2011

Sony commissioned KDa to reconceive the design of its retail stores in the Americas. Sony wanted a friendly and vibrant design that created a system that could unify its many stores while being flexible enough to adjust to local conditions. The first store was completed in Los Angeles, and KDa's design has been rolled out internationally.

Needing to ensure construction was straightforward for the global rollout, the shell of the interior is simple. However, through the cunning use of color, standardization, and relocatable elements, KDa has invested the store with fun and intelligence. The store's sidewalls have been lined with a standardized system of colorful, fabric-covered acoustic panels that can be quickly reconfigured to suit changing marketing requirements or even seasons—the red panels can be moved to the front of the store at Christmas time! The furniture has been designed around a clever new system of display "tiles." Topped with a removable graphic and designed with holes that keep wires out of sight, the tiles can be quickly moved around or replaced, allowing Sony HQ to guide the way products are displayed and giving the flexibility to rearrange the tiles as new products arrive in store.

Personal Computers
VAIO
VAIO
/map/launch/discover/
VAIO
VAIO
VAIO

SONY

Personal Audio

blip.tv
blip.tv
blip.tv
SONY
NEX-3 & 5
pocket professionals
NEX-3 & 5
Which is for you?
NEX-3 & 5
E-mount interchangeable lens

"A chandelier with 10,000 Swarovski crystals sparkles"

SHISEIDO THE GINZA

Tokyo, Japan // Retail // 856 m²
Shiseido // 2011

Located in Tokyo's glamorous Ginza shopping district, Shiseido the Ginza is a flagship store for legendary Japanese cosmetics company Shiseido. The store occupies the lower three floors of a new tower, each floor having its own character and emphasizing different products and services.

At street level, KDa wanted to create a space that was as open, welcoming and fun as possible. KDa conceived the space as a marketplace in a town square, surrounded by an arcade where individual shops face onto the square. Evoking the baskets of fruit and vegetables found in a town market, more than 2,000 Shiseido products are displayed in boxes made from many different materials.

On the second floor, the arches turn into cabinets reminiscent of an old pharmacy. Here, personal consultation is provided in a more sober atmosphere. This floor includes a professional hair and makeup salon as well as a photography studio—after customers have had their hair and make-up done, they can be photographed by an in-house photographer.

On the third floor, the arches follow the layout of a monastic cloister, where a chandelier with 10,000 Swarovski crystals sparkles over a display of Shiseido's top-of-the-line products. Here the atmosphere is a moody, low-lit, chapel-like ambience; the dark blue walls and ceiling are a perfect setting for a serene and relaxing spa treatment.

"The elephant in the room"

ARTEK MEETS DOVER STREET MARKET

Tokyo, Japan // Installation // 61 m²
Artek // 2013

To celebrate the sixtieth anniversary of Alvar Aalto's iconic Artek stool, KDa was invited to design an installation at the Dover Street Market Gallery in Ginza. The gallery features a permanent art fixture—a life-sized elephant—that all exhibitors must incorporate into their work.

Together with Artek, KDa designed new stools with differing heights, the green legs becoming blades of grass, evoking the image of the elephant standing among swaying savannah grasses. The playful twist? The stools double as steps, inviting visitors to climb up and take a seat on the elephant's towering golden Artek stool!

"A gin and tonic-like agency"

BEACON COMMUNICATIONS OFFICE

Tokyo, Japan // Office // 5,230 m²
Beacon Communications // 2002

The brief for Beacon, a cutting-edge advertising agency, was spiritedly poetic. It asked for its interior renovations to be like mixing "a gin and tonic." It had to be flavorful but clear and transparent, fizz with effervescence but be cool as ice, be fun like a dash of alcohol, zesty as a slice of lime, and maintain the edge of tonic water.

The challenge was to devise a striking but practical way to divide Beacon's narrow and linear floor spaces into private areas for staff and public areas for clients. Following the shape of the slender building, a single element was used on each floor: a long undulating ribbon that wrapped around functional spaces to form continuous walls, floors and ceilings.

Within the loops and arcs of the ribbons, small private rooms, including napping pods, a kitchen, and relaxation areas, were created. Flanking these cozy sections were open-plan work areas for staff. Entrances on either side of the ribbons—one for employees, the other for clients—ensured the private rooms would remain unseen by the public.

Each floor's ribbon was color-coded to represent Beacon's advertising expertise. Pink snakeskin curled around spaces designed for consultations with cosmetic, toiletries, and beauty product clients. Tobacco, car manufacturers, and technology clients would find themselves within blue arches, while green represented family-oriented industries.

As an advertising business, where sharing ideas is essential to the creative process, Beacon also required spaces that encouraged social interaction and communication. Cubicles and personal offices were replaced with an extended table at which any employee could work side by side with directors. An amphitheater, and open-plan meeting and innovation lab spaces were added within the ribbons for presentations and consultations.

At a time when the popularity of open-plan offices was relatively new, Beacon's balance of privacy and openness, playful curved aesthetics, and warm colors brought a coziness to the office that anticipated another trend: the focus on work-life balance that we see today.

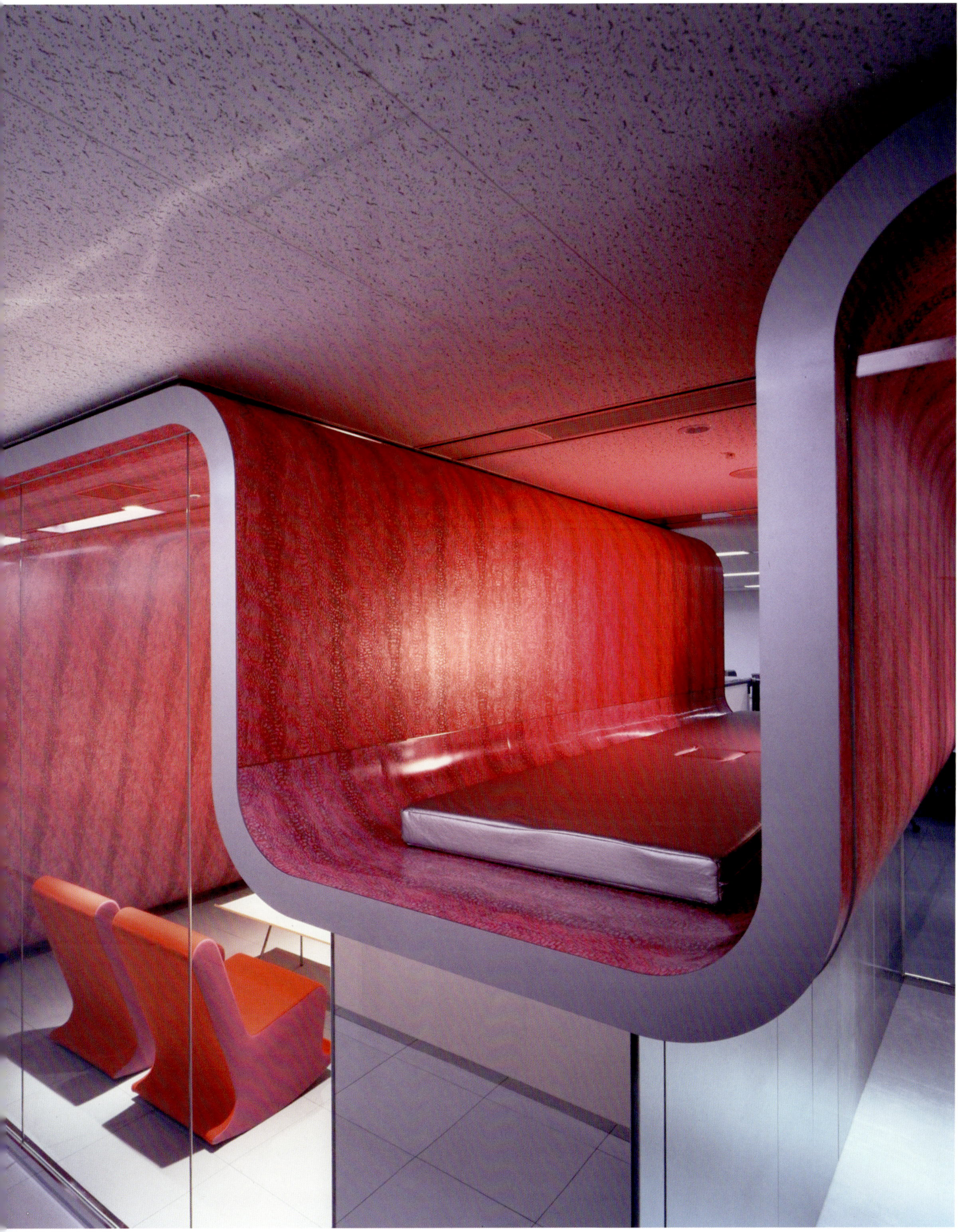

"I'll meet you in the hairy kitchen"

GOOGLE JAPAN

Tokyo, Japan // Office // 3,219 m²
Google Japan // 2010

KDa completed an additional phase to their design for Google's Japan office. This ambitious interior project is located in the Roppongi Hills tower in central Tokyo.

In such a large project, one of the key challenges was to develop a way to expand Google's facilities that wasn't repetitive or boring, and which also assisted wayfinding. To help staff feel comfortable and prevent visitors from becoming lost, KDa defined various zones across the floors and gave each a distinct character. Each zone was assigned a specific color, the colors being modulated through different tones. This created a "necklace" of differently colored meeting rooms, each with a specific name and character, strung around the building's large central core.

On one of the floors, KDa defined the circuitous route around the meeting rooms with the perforated concrete block walls common in Tokyo's winding residential lanes. In the city, these block walls often provide glimpses into lush gardens, and KDa used them here to allow views into enticing spaces. Each of these "pocket parks" has a huge wall graphic of brightly colored plants and can be used for gatherings and informal meetings.

KDa also placed landmarks at key positions to help staff and visitors identify their location and navigate around the floor. Mini-kitchens each have a different color theme. After having designed kitchens themed by Google colors—blue, yellow, red, green—on the lower floors, KDa looked to create something even more memorable: a bright blue "hairy kitchen" clad in the giant brushes used in automatic carwashes.

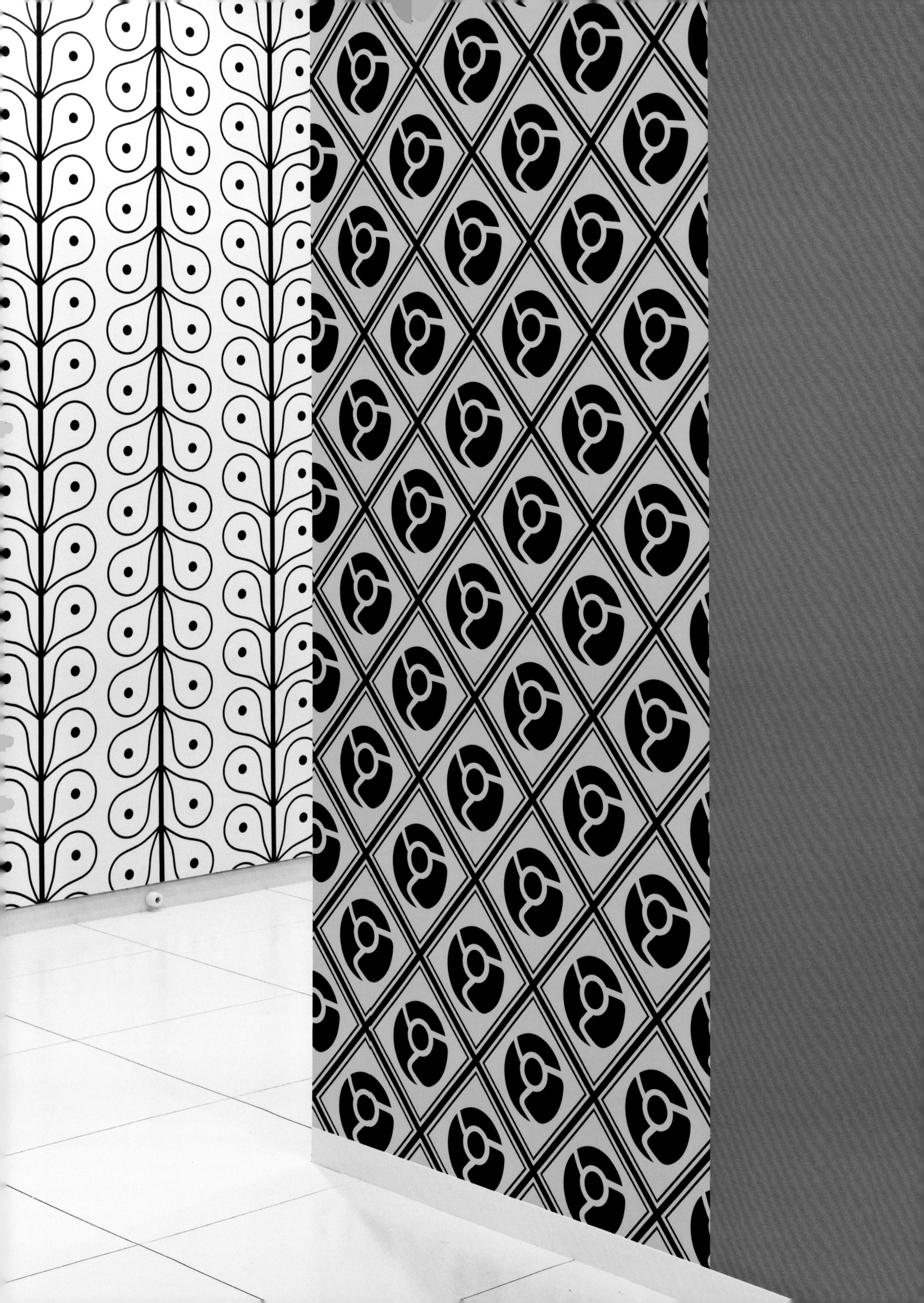

A set of spaces on another floor was themed after a *sento*, the traditional neighborhood bathhouses now fast disappearing from Japan's cities. Passing through a traditional *noren* curtain leads to a space instantly recognizable as a "wash area", complete with white ceramic tiles, wooden stools, and computer screens cunningly configured where mirrors would be expected. This leads on to a spacious "soaking bath" area—actually a presentation and training room—which, like classic *sento*, features a huge mural of Mount Fuji specially created for Google by one of Japan's last living *sento* mural painters. This space is also used for external events, with the "wash area" becoming a reception space for drinks. Nearby, a group of meeting rooms have a *matsuri* (traditional neighborhood festival) theme. Here, red and orange wallpaper picks up patterns from the *yukata* robes and *happi* coats worn at festivals, wall graphics show photos of festival scenes, and sake and beer crates act as impromptu seating and create a relaxed party atmosphere.

For other sections of the interior, KDa created brightly colored wallpaper patterns cleverly derived from refigured Google icons, such as the Google Android and Google Map pin. For the new spaces, KDa developed a set of muted, timber-colored wall graphics with tones varying from light to dark wood. Subtly evoking Japan's traditional timber architecture, the patterns occasionally incorporate cunningly hidden icons.

Each of Google's national offices around the world reflects the culture of its location. KDa's design for the earlier phases of the project had taken cues from the graphics of traditional Japanese fabrics and contemporary animé, but then Google requested an even more vivid evocation of Japanese culture. Looking to communicate the Japanese context without resorting to clichés, KDa incorporated surprising elements such as a full-scale *yatai* (mobile food stall) and a digital koi pond that greets people at one of the entrances—responding to hidden sensors, carp projected onto the floor move toward those who enter the space as if expecting to be fed.

"Just click 'Play'"

YOUTUBE SPACE TOKYO

Tokyo, Japan // Studio // 605 m²
YouTube // 2013

YouTube Space Tokyo includes studios, production suites, training areas, and lounges, and serves as a collaborative production facility intended to help the website's most energetic producers elevate their videos to a professional level.

Located high in the Mori Tower in central Tokyo, KDa's layout is organized around a visually striking wall of red panels derived from YouTube's distinctive logo, while another wall serves as a hall of fame, showing images of the top producers. The space has been arranged to maximize the use of the iconic Tokyo Tower skyline as a shooting backdrop. Features include a super-long curtain partition and rearrangeable furniture, as well as the variety of wall surfaces, carpet shades, and ceiling configurations intended to provide a wide range of shooting settings.

YouTube

YouTube Space
TOKYO 東京

"Let's meet in the *horigotatsu*"

BARTLE BOGLE HEGARTY

Tokyo, Japan // Office // 426 m²
Bartle Bogle Hegarty // 1998

The client, an internationally well-known advertising company, required a striking interior befitting its image for its Tokyo branch, located in a standard office building. It was soon to expand and move to a larger space in a couple of years' time. Therefore, the idea was to focus on the furniture that could be moved in the future. The walls and ceiling were left untouched as they would have to be returned to their initial state when moving out.

The rectangular office is a modest size and, in order to give an impression of space, a simple linear layout was used. The meeting space was to reflect Japanese culture in some way, so the small private room is in the shape of a U with a sunken table, or *horigotatsu* in Japanese. The U seems to hover above the bright red floor and guests have to take their shoes off to step onto the elevated meeting space. A silver curtain ensures privacy as well as allowing for darkened TV viewing or slide projection.

The desks and central filing cabinet take the shape of an upside-down U. All have a polished UV lacquer finish. Standard anglepoise lights fixed to the furniture ensure cozy individual lighting compared with the exposed fluorescent ceiling lights.

Bartle Bogle Hegarty
BARTLE BOGLE HEGARTY LTD

"More green, clearer mind"

POINT 0 MARUNOUCHI

Tokyo, Japan // Coworking space // 1,087 m²
Point 0 // 2019

A complete renovation of a fourth-floor office in Tokyo's business district of Marunouchi, Point 0 is Japan's first coworking space to be awarded a Gold Level International WELL Building Institute certification. It combines lush indoor greenery with a wealth of therapeutic amenities, including a coffee bar, private nap and shower rooms, focus booths, a meditation room, and work zones.

More than twenty companies share Point 0, many of whom collaborated on its interiors and high-tech fittings. This makes the space not only a haven of beneficial work experiences, but also a cohesive showroom of local industry prowess and experimentation. When it opened in 2019, its combination of nature and technology anticipated an evolution in office spaces that we see continuing today.

On entering Point 0, employees pass through a cleaning portal where an electrostatic device removes city dust and other allergens. Inside, the coworking space opens out to a spacious, wood-toned communal area where employees can mingle and work from desk or lounge chairs. Daylight is filtered by the foliage of a long window-side arboretum. Below, a stretch of wooden benches offers casual seating in the shade of the leafy boughs. Fertile planters overflow with vines, their tendrils cascading over steel framework shelves, adding to the space's intentional greenhouse aesthetic.

For presentations and events, the communal area can be divided or closed off by a sweeping green curtain. The steel framework shelving system is also modular. Custom-made furniture offers flexible storage, display units and extra countertops.

Individual meeting rooms flank the communal space, each carpeted and divided by panels of stone-colored terrazzo. A corridor along the east side features illustrations of trees and shelves to display collaborating companies' exhibits, visible from the glass-paneled meeting rooms. Tucked away at the far end of the corridor lie areas for contemplation, focus, and recuperation—a tatami mat meditation room complete with a mini rock garden, focus booths with wafts of cool air, three shower cubicles, and two cozy nap rooms.

"Scattered across this landscape is a miniature village"

TBWA\HAKUHODO

Tokyo, Japan // Office // 4,215 m²
TBWA\Hakuhodo // 2007

This project is the Tokyo HQ of a joint venture between TBWA, an innovative global advertising agency, and Hakuhodo, one of Japan's largest advertising firms, and was built in a disused bowling alley that KDa discovered in a multi-story amusement complex. KDa conceived of the office interior as a park and filled it with plants, boardwalks and green shag-pile carpet. Scattered across this landscape is a miniature village. Individual shelters serve as meeting rooms, project rooms, and directors' offices, and some have been fitted with ladders that allow staff to climb onto their roofs to find a relaxed spot for meetings or a break. The bowling alley's column-free space allowed the office to be laid out freely, but the building's bowling lane DNA showed through in the down-stand beams on the ceiling, so this dynamic was incorporated to give a subtle order to the layout of the office landscape.

"Before you fly, soak in the animé and bamboo"

VIRGIN ATLANTIC: THE CLUBHOUSE

Narita, Japan // Airport lounge // 190 m²
Virgin Atlantic // 2007

Virgin Atlantic tailors each of its airline lounges to reflect the character of its host city. The brief for Virgin's new Clubhouse at Tokyo's Narita Airport was to embody equal parts Virgin, Japan, KDa. The goal was to create a comfortable, inviting space where travelers could relax before their flight—whether by unwinding in a lounge chair, plugging in their laptops, or catching up on the news.

To define the different relaxation zones, KDa designed a series of "fin screens" that offer clear views of the runway when viewed head-on, but function as light partitions when seen from an angle. Each fin features a dual-sided design: one side is printed with a traditional bamboo scene, while the other showcases contemporary animé imagery from Koji Morimoto, known for *The Animatrix*. Upon entering the lounge, visitors encounter the traditional side, but as they move toward the kitchen counter and glance back, they are met with a vision of the future. This juxtaposition of past and future reflects the many cultural ambiguities that define Japan—contrasts that KDa sought to capture within the lounge's design.

"PokoPoko reminds us of a cozy spot in a fairy tale"

POKOPOKO, RISONARE NASU

Nasu, Japan // Clubhouse // 299 m²
Hoshino Resorts // 2019

Nasu Highlands, in the northern corner of Tochigi Prefecture, can be reached in 75 minutes by bullet train from Tokyo. This cluster of volcanic mountains is home to some of the region's premier hot springs and their most regular visitors: monkeys.

PokoPoko was born from a client's wish to connect two hotel buildings on the current site. The vision included an extension and renovation of both buildings and rooms, the original smaller guest house from 1986, and its later addition, bringing the total number of rooms on-site to thirty.

Working with landscape design Studio Terra, KDa created a new path meandering through the lush forest as a subtle connection between the two complexes.

Halfway along the path is a fairy-tale-like contemporary cottage located in a clearing of the woods. Lighthearted, human-scale, and iconic, it catches the eye from afar. The building takes its name from the Japanese onomatopoeia for popping up: PokoPoko.

The newly created building is a family-oriented clubhouse and activity center for all the hotel guests. For guests walking through the forest, PokoPoko stands out with its three conical roofs, which emerge from three circular, slightly intersecting base plans. Each has its own specific character.

The central cone hosts cooking activities based on lots of fresh vegetables and herbs, all grown in the hotel's own farm garden. The variety of food-related workshops allows kids and adults to prepare their own jams and pickles, while a big wood oven offers an opportunity to make pizza using vegetables and spices just picked from the on-site garden.

Floor plan

To one side, the adjacent cone houses an open fireplace around which KDa placed its own designed doradora modular seating system. The circular configuration of the furniture elements in green tones feels welcoming and inclusive. The hotel guests can gather around the fireplace, relax with a cup of tea or glass of wine, read a book, gaze into the flames, or simply enjoy the 360-degree view to the surrounding trees. PokoPoko brings the forest into the space, making visitors feel like they spent a day in nature even on a rainy day. On the inside, it invites guests to look up, past the wooden structure through to the circular skylight toward the sky.

On the other side of the central cone, the space is dedicated to kids. A big climbing net with a ball pit at the bottom spans the entire internal structure of this unit. The indoor playground offers the freedom to rest in the upper section of the net, or endlessly climb up and down. Kids can release energy even when the weather is too gloomy to play outside, but if it's fine, they can toast marshmallows on the campfire on the round decks out front.

The material palette highlights simple and natural materials, both on the exterior and interior. PokoPoko is a cozy spot in nature where inside and outside, lively and peaceful, are flowing from one space to another in playful harmony.

"Lift the veil for a kiss"

LEAF CHAPEL, RISONARE YATSUGATAKE

Kobuchizawa, Japan // Wedding chapel // 167 m²
Hoshino Resorts // 2004

The Leaf Chapel sits within the grounds of the Risonare Yatsugatake resort in Kobuchizawa, a refreshingly green setting with beautiful views to the southern Japanese Alps, Yatsugatake peaks and Mount Fuji.

The chapel is formed of two leaves—one glass, one steel—which have seemingly fluttered to the ground.

The glass leaf with its delicate lace-pattern motif emulates a pergola, and the structure holding it up reminds one of the veins of a leaf, which slowly become thinner the further they get from the central stem.

The white steel leaf, perforated with 4,700 holes, each of which holds an acrylic lens, is similar to a bride's veil made of delicate lace. Light filters through the lenses and projects a lace pattern onto the white fabric inside. Throughout the day as the sun turns, the projected pattern naturally changes to create myriad different lace patterns on the inner lining of the veil, revealing a marvelous backdrop to the wedding ceremony.

At the end of the ceremony, when the groom lifts the bride's veil for the traditional kiss, the "steel veil" magically opens too, revealing the pond and the enchanting nature beyond. Although weighing 11 tons, a hydraulic system allows the veil to lift silently, almost like a piece of fabric, in 38 seconds.

The bright white purity of the occasion is heightened even more by keeping the interior materials purposely dark, so that the bride and the kimono-wearing guests stand out while the men in black suits fade into the background; the side walls are clad in blackened timber and the floor laid in black granite. Black timber benches can accommodate a party of up to eighty people.

The backrests of the benches are made of cast acrylic. A light green flower motif is encapsulated in the 20-millimeter acrylic, giving the pattern a somewhat soft and fluid effect. When seen from the back of the chapel and against the pond through the open veil, the impression is of many water plants blooming in the pond; or when the veil is down, a flower field, which seems to sway in front of the white background.

The flower chosen is a rempukusou, a rather petite flower with yellow petals, which grows at a stream nearby; however, the Chinese characters of its name signify good luck, befitting happy weddings!

At the end of the ceremony, when the veil is up, the wedding party carefully walks on the stepping stones across the pond to where the lawn surrounded by trees welcomes them for the champagne toast.

A moonlight wedding ceremony at the Leaf Chapel can be dramatic, too, as a warm floodlight shines through the acrylic lenses of the veil revealing yet another astonishing lace pattern. On the lifting of the veil, a sea of candles awaits the guests on the lawn across the pond. And while they sip their champagne, the Leaf Chapel sets the mood in the background. With the veil closed and light shining from the inside, the chapel becomes a huge yet delicate lantern.

Japanese Construction

There is a concept in Japanese culture known as *monozukuri* that helps explain why it is such a pleasure to practice architecture in Japan. Though the literal translation of *monozukuri* is "making things," the term implies so much more. It embodies the spirit of craftsmanship that underpins the nation's manufacturing industries—a philosophy of meticulous workmanship, continuous improvement and the pursuit of perfection.

Integral to this are surprisingly close collaborations between architects, manufacturers, construction companies, and engineers. To regularly visit factories and meet engineers and other key personnel is an essential part of the process. It's also one of the greatest joys of working in Japan, something that nurtures friendships as well as professional relationships.

On the factory floor, architects get to see cutting-edge technology and new materials firsthand, while witnessing the precision and care taken to manufacture components. Discussions with collaborators often lead to revelations and innovations that would not have surfaced otherwise, and the level of enthusiasm to embrace challenges and experimentation is palpable.

To create the sliding veil of the Leaf Chapel in Kobuchizawa in Yamanashi Prefecture, KDa approached a company that specializes in enormous retractable stadium domes. The company was not only willing to produce a miniature version of its complex mechanisms but also reveled in the novelty of constructing something so tiny. From start to finish, KDa was invited to observe the progress, from sheets of metal being pressed in factories to their arrival and construction on-site. Attention to detail was impeccable; timing and delivery flawless. When some trucks reached Kobuchizawa early, they paused nearby and waited for the others to ensure they would all drive in procession at precisely 8 am.

One of the best examples of such an elevated level of prowess and conscientiousness occurred after the Leaf Chapel was completed. When a mysterious faint knocking sound was heard each time its roof opened and closed, a specialist was sent to investigate. Arriving on a Harley Davidson like a mounted hero, he walked around the structure, intently listening as the roof was operated. Then he simply said, "The bearings need to be moved by 2 degrees."

The bearings were shifted, and the sound completely disappeared. The specialist straddled his bike to ride off into what can only be imagined as the sunset.

FUSO

"It magically disappears into the forest"

BRILLARE, RISONARE YATSUGATAKE

Kobuchizawa, Japan // Wedding reception venue // 124 m²
Hoshino Resorts // 2005

Brillare, a striking wedding reception space, takes its name from the Italian word for "shining." Two hours' drive from Tokyo, it shimmers like a vision within a serene forest glade of the luxury hotel.

Brillare extends Hoshino Resorts' Risonare Yatsugatake's intimate wedding villa into nature, and invites guests to celebrate and feast within the romantic ambience of a verdant grove. It completes a unique wedding experience that begins with KDa's visionary Leaf Chapel.

Sliding floor-to-ceiling glass panels run the entire length of the reception hall, drawing in natural light and opening to views of dense woodland. Central to the room is an 18-meter-long communal table. A ceramic tiled floor matches the all-white interiors that reflect and enhance the light within the space. Above, an elegant silhouette of a leafy vine unfurls across the ceiling and around a constellation of spotlights, to cascade behind the wedding couple at the head of the table.

Minimalism is balanced by an intriguing play on perspective. The banquet table is gently tapered. This allows the newlyweds to see the faces of all their guests, but also visually extends the table to stretch into the distance. For guests, the happy couple appear closer, larger than life and the absolute center of attention.

The exterior of Brillare echoes its interior optical illusion. Cantilevered, the angled structure seems to hover. Seen from different standpoints, the reflections of trees in its mirror-polished steel cladding shift like an otherworldly camouflage. As night falls, the reflections fade, and the room and its guests become a glowing tableau of festivity suspended in the forest.

"Bathing in the woods"

MOKU MOKU YU, RISONARE YATSUGATAKE

Kobuchizawa, Japan // Bathhouse // 488 m²
Hoshino Resorts // 2006

Moku Moku Yu is a timber bathhouse set amid pine forest at the Risonare Yatsugatake resort, site of a number of other KDa interventions.

Communal bathing is an ancient and venerable tradition in Japan. How to do something that feels right for the ritual, without imitating the usual treatment? How to create something fresh in such well-worked territory?

"Bathing together, in a wooden barrel, under the trees, in the snow!" In this image, KDa found the answer to the architectural dilemmas—use circles! The interpenetration of spaces serves to blur the usual divisions between inside and outside, and between male and female. Bathers separate by sex at the entrance for undressing and washing, but are able to rejoin in the outdoor communal bath (*konyoku rotenburo*).

There is something both comforting and tantalizing about these intersecting round rooms. The hierarchy, axis, and orientation of linear plans are replaced by local centers, embracing curves and a subtle sense of motion. Rather than responding to the linear functionalist thinking, this bathhouse aims for a series of linked states of being.

"A sanctuary for dragonflies and ice skaters"

PICCHIO VISITORS CENTRE

Karuizawa, Japan // Visitor center, café, ice rink // 85 m²
Hoshino Resorts // 2016

Picchio Visitors Centre is located in the foothills of Mount Asama, an active volcano. This area of Japan, known as Karuizawa, is famous for its hot springs, cool temperatures in the summer months, red leaves in autumn, and snow in the winter, making it the perfect weekend retreat from Tokyo, which is only 90 minutes away by bullet train. The structure acts as a skating clubhouse in winter and a nature center in the summer.

The center is next to Japan's first bird sanctuary, which was established in 1964 along with a simple square ice rink. The bird sanctuary emerged as a breeding ground for dragonflies—a huge attraction for visitors in summer.

A large curved double-sided bench runs down the center of the space, allowing people to face the pond in the summer with the doors fully open. The other side faces shelves with research materials, displays and monitors. The space widens toward one end for informal talks and workshops. In winter the double-sided bench gives ample space for lacing up skates, or watching the swirling skaters outside. The building is cleverly placed so that spectators and skaters alike can soak up the winter sun on a fine day.

A third of the rink has cooling pipes to help freeze the ice nearest the clubhouse; as the temperatures decrease, people can skate around the whole rink. This may be the first time in the world an ice rink has combined both assisted freezing and natural ice.

Huge efforts were made to both echo and respect the natural features of the site. Two deep wintering pools were made in the pond so that fish could have a place where the ice did not fully freeze, and the natural flow of the water was the guide for landscaping. To ensure that even in the depths of winter there is always a hint of the summer months to come, brightly colored aluminum panels among the cedar shingles bring to mind the iridescent dragonfly eyes that will surely return to the pond as temperatures rise.

"A beach in the sky"

SORA NO BEACH, RISONARE ATAMI

Atami, Japan // Hotel // 10,106 m²
Hoshino Resorts // 2011

Atami is a resort town located on a spectacular stretch of coastline an hour by bullet train from Tokyo. Its main attractions are its seaside location and hot springs that feed the town's many *onsen* baths. It also holds fireworks festivals once a month, almost all year round. It's a great place for Tokyo-ites to spend an easy, fun weekend away.

KDa has refurbished a huge hotel on the steep slopes overlooking the town. Designed for Hoshino Resorts, this project follows on from a series of projects, which includes the Leaf Chapel, Brillare and The Tomamu Towers.

Constructed in the 1980s, the original hotel was a monument to the glitz and extravagance of the "Bubble Era." Oversized rooms and sprawling buildings meant the hotel was overwhelming to visit and difficult to run. Hoshino's ambition was to reposition Risonare Atami as a family-oriented hotel with great facilities and fun activities for kids, as happy kids mean relaxed parents.

One of the first significant changes was Sora no Beach, or the Sky Beach. Though the hotel is set high above Atami's actual beach, KDa ingeniously brought the beach experience to the hotel itself. A café and lounge were designed with natural sand, giving guests an indoor-outdoor beach vibe. Visitors enter along a wooden boardwalk, where they can browse books, relax at the café bar, or kick off their shoes and enjoy the sandy "beach." Sun loungers and cabanas enhance the beachy feel, while expansive terraces allow guests to soak up the sun—and enjoy the spectacular fireworks displays from a prime vantage point.

"A cascading burst of fireworks"

HANABI RESTAURANT, RISONARE ATAMI

Atami, Japan // Hotel // 10,106 m²
Hoshino Resorts // 2011

Given the prominence of fireworks in Atami's culture, it was only natural for KDa to weave this theme into one of the restaurants at Risonare Atami. Fireworks, symbolic of the town's festive spirit, inspired the creation of an intimate, immersive dining experience. In any restaurant, there is a need to break up large spaces to create a more personal, human scale. What better way to do this than by evoking the gentle, falling sparks of fireworks to define each dining area?

KDa designed a series of filigree firework structures that serve as delicate spatial dividers within the restaurant. These intricate, radial steel structures are designed in various sizes to accommodate tables for two, four or six guests, creating a sense of privacy without feeling confined. The steel rods radiate from a central point and are painted with a gradient, mimicking the way fireworks change color as they descend. To heighten the illusion of movement, KDa designed the steel piping to break in certain areas, reinforcing the sensation of sparks gently falling from a firework burst.

The walls of the restaurant are adorned with floor-to-ceiling prints of Atami's iconic fireworks, captured by one of Japan's most renowned fireworks photographers. These vibrant images bring the explosive beauty of the town's firework displays indoors, complementing the subtle, metallic structures and adding depth to the atmosphere. Together, the filigree fireworks and the striking prints transport diners into a world where they are not just spectators, but participants in the spectacle of light and celebration that defines Atami.

This combination of intimate design and visual storytelling turns a simple meal into a magical, sensory experience.

"Room with a view"

BERGMANN RESIDENCE

Hakone, Japan // Residential // 283 m²
Nicolai Bergmann // 2018

Sequestered on the north-facing side of Mount Hakone, the Bergmann Residence, a mountain villa built for Danish flower artist Nicolai Bergmann, is enveloped by the beauty of nature. Green forests abound, while in the distance, sulfurous mists drift over the volcanic terrain of Owakudani valley.

The residence takes its cues from these environs, transforming the challenges of its location within Fuji Hakone Izu National Park into an architectural dialogue with the wilderness.

Elevated on four stepped platforms, the Bergmann Residence's ascending structure echoes the hillside it rests on; the space beneath is left hollow to allow mountain water runoff to flow below and into a meandering garden brook. National-park building regulations—a mandatory pitched roof, limited glass glazing, and color restrictions—were all adapted into architectural features designed to blend into the landscape.

The roof is low sloped, its underside clad in oak slats that seamlessly extend into the building to form a timber ceiling. It becomes a striking floating roof, hovering over front-facing window walls, yet when viewed head-on, it appears unobtrusively flat, disguising the upper floor that lies behind it. A sunken living room at the front and a central dining/kitchen area offer panoramic views of tree-topped mountain peaks, while a raised lounge at the back intimately faces a leafy knoll. A guest bedroom and laundry room are tucked away in corners, while upstairs, family quarters are hidden behind the slope of the roof.

Inspired by Bergmann's love of Japan and Denmark and their overlapping aesthetics, the selected colors and textures reflect those of nature. Outside, black yaki-sugi (burnt pine) gable cladding is tempered by muted gray textured concrete sidewalls and earthy Ippei wood decking. Inside, Danish oak is used throughout in subtle contrasts of natural tones and rich dark floorboards.

Bergmann's own creativity completes the residence, transforming the garden with his personal landscaping vision.

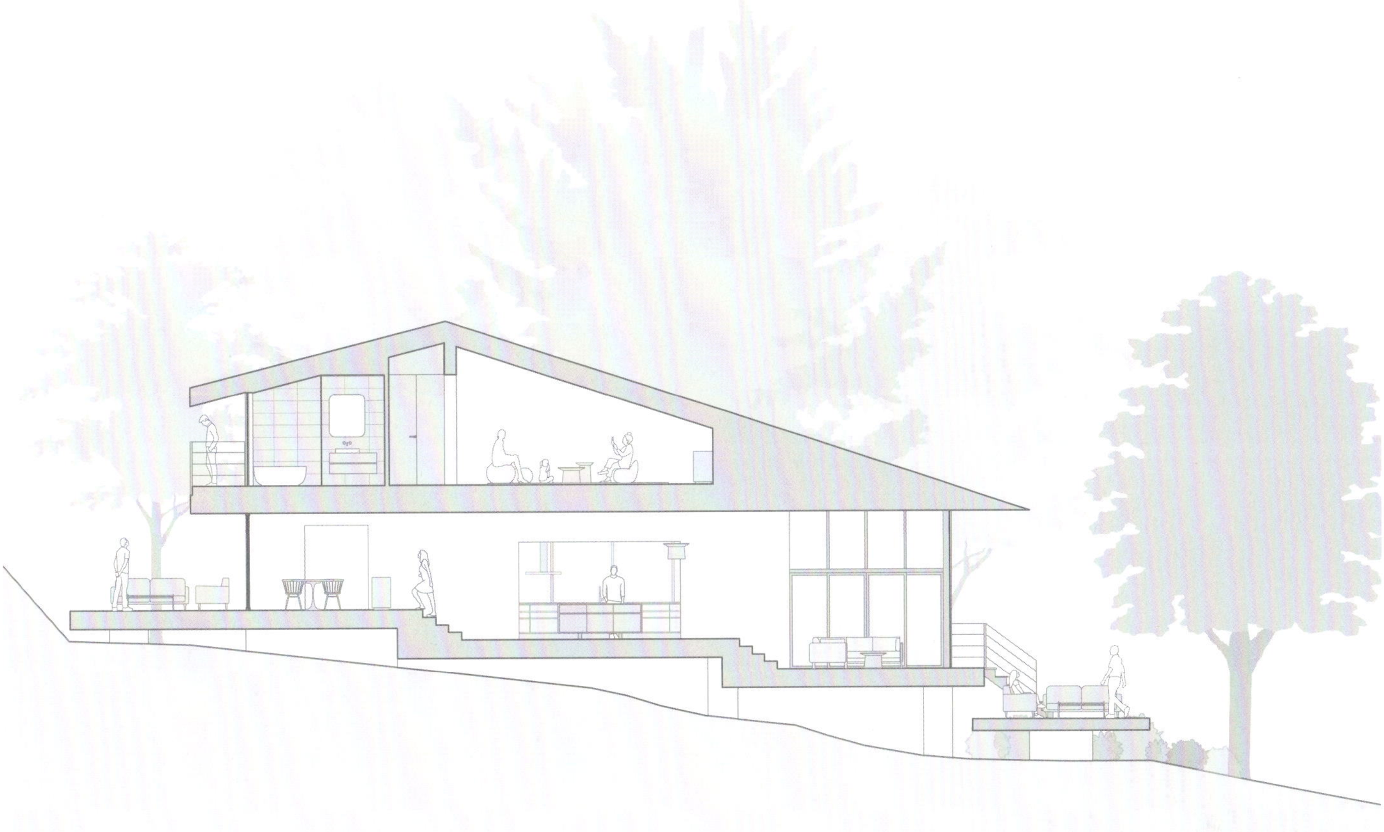

Section

"A music box in the woods"

RIE HOUSE

Karuizawa, Japan // Residential // 139 m²
Private // 2023

Surrounded by leafy woodland in Karuizawa, Rie House is built on a picturesque knoll that was once home to a summer villa. Its residents, a family, requested a modest but unique dwelling that would accommodate a creative lifestyle and reflect their artistic and musical personalities.

A new, two-story structure, Rie House follows the hillside, the folds of its pitched roof echoing the land's natural slope. Its metal-clad exterior is monotone—a cheerful mint-green from roof peak to wall base that stands out among the trees. A funnel-shaped entrance opens outward like a trumpet, inviting guests into a vivid, sunny yellow porch.

Inside, the sloped ceiling enhances a double-height central living, kitchen and dining space of warm, minimalist wooden interiors—a blank canvas in which the owners can express themselves. Rie House's location on a gentle slope allows the open-plan living area to lead into a split-level, lower music room housing the owners' grand piano, guitars, and other instruments. An interior balcony overlooks all, connecting the top floor of two bedrooms and creating a visual flow between the home's three levels. Beneath the bedrooms, a guest room, the bathroom and a study occupy the more enclosed first-floor spaces.

When completed, the residents' grandmother, who owned the old summer home that stood before Rie House was built, gave the ultimate compliment. She was so delighted with the bright and joyful transformation of the land, she immediately offered to buy her granddaughter any extra furnishing to complete the family's vision.

"A white house in the city"

SASAO HOUSE

Tokyo, Japan // Residential // 193 m²
Private // 2011

Just a few blocks from Tokyo's ultramodern high-rises, Sasao House's white, faceted structure stands out in the backstreets of Nishi Shinjuku like an architectural gemstone. Wrapped from roof to ground in diamond-shaped metal shingles, its textured façade folds over the building, enhancing its unusual angular form with subtle diagonal lines.

A neighborhood landmark in the friendly residential area, Sasao House is a compact multi-generational home combined with the family's business, a popular *tonkatsu* (fried pork cutlet) restaurant by day and lively bar by night. The first floor meets the street curb to welcome visitors to its cozy eatery, the second floor serves as an apartment for the client's parents, while the third floor and a rooftop room house the client's family of three. It stands on a corner where annual *matsuri* festival parades stop to take a break, and the family, all active members of the local community, requested a building that would be a striking backdrop to the colorful traditional floats.

In a sense, Sasao House designed itself. Located on temple-owned land, rented and lived on for generations by the same family, its irregular pentagonal prism form takes full advantage of the site's corner plot dimensions. The unconventional angles of its façade were dictated by shadow lines to ensure the street it stands on receives direct sunlight. Its sloping roof maximizes vertical space to conceal a spacious loft bedroom that faces an open terrace. Windows of different sizes dot the façade to mask the building's scale and maintain privacy. Behind, the terrace allows daylight to flood through a glass wall to illuminate the double-height living room of the apartment below. Throughout, interiors are crisp white to reflect and maximize light, aside from a single colorful floral accent wall—a reflection of the vibrant personalities of its residents.

煮

KOWKA
明日
PLAY SNACK
万季

12
山京
SAPPORO
炭火やきとり
鳥駒
3227-3187
せんば

"From doodle to façade"

SIN DEN

Tokyo, Japan // Beauty salon, house // 99 m^2
Yamamotokougyou // 2007

Between the vanguard fashion boutiques of Harajuku and the elegant stores of Aoyama, Sin Den sits within the quieter streets of Jingumae, a residential neighborhood of local individuality and its own pockets of inspired creativity. Designed for a young couple and their baby, this unusual project combines a compact home with the family's cutting-edge hairdressing business—all within a 50-square-meter site.

Sin Den's huge black box structure—a first floor and basement hair salon, and two upper residential floors—is informed by repeated studies in height and massing to ensure maximum and efficient use of space. The façade of its monumental form features bold, white linework delineating the Sin Den logo: a woman's upturned face framed by her flowing hair. Behind her, an explosion of floral filigree unfurls over windows and wraps around the structure like the sprawling ivy of neighboring buildings. Contrary to the strong external appearance, the interior is softer, an ideal setting for a family home. Surfaces are clad in organic colors and lit by ample natural light from large windows.

By day, Sin Den is a dramatic, 3D, and intriguing mural. Part artwork, part billboard, it draws attention to the hair salon's slightly hidden location. At night, it becomes residential and intimate, its square windows puncturing the graphic design with the soft glow of the building's interior.

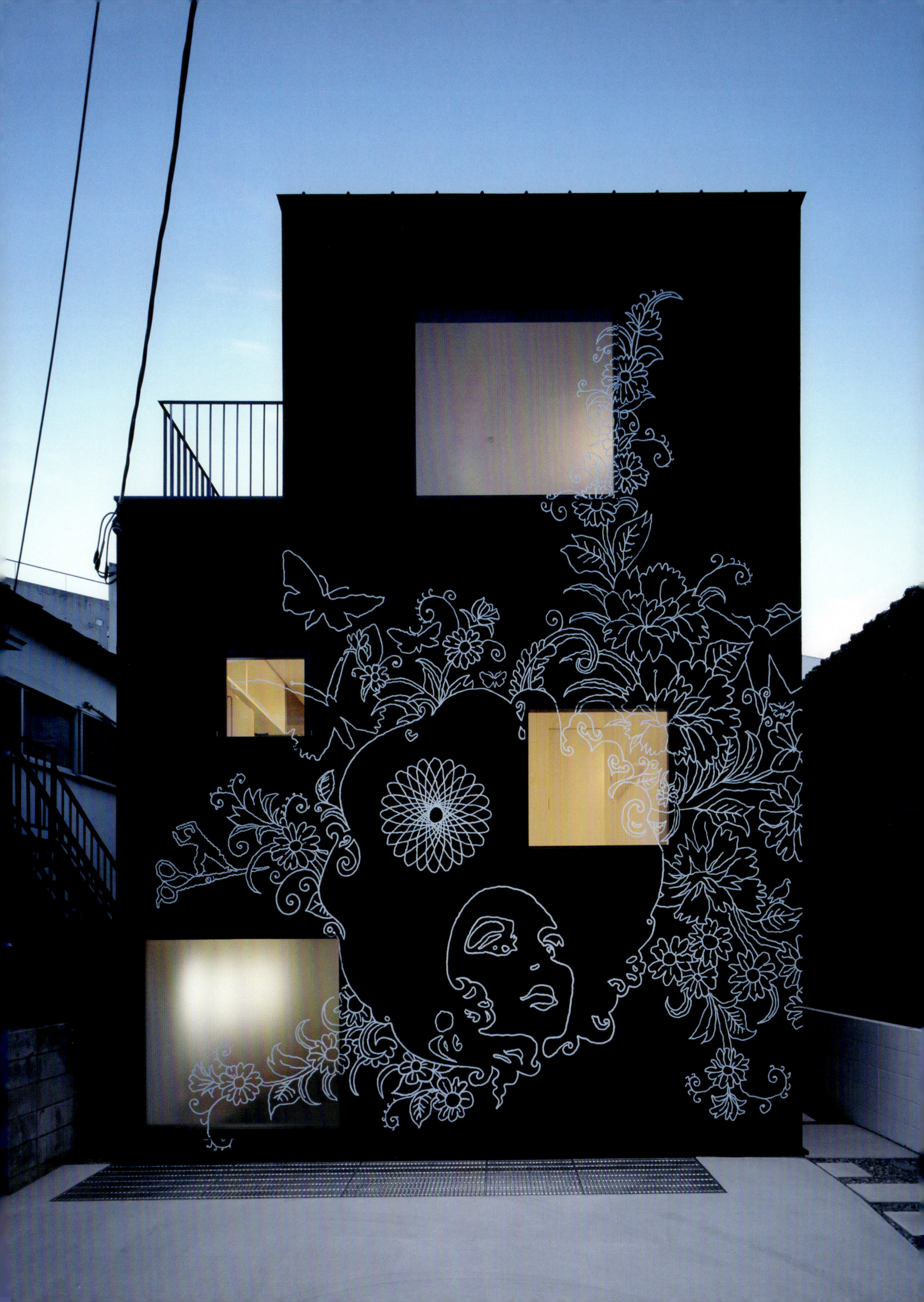

"Car cave"

VROOOM!

Nagoya, Japan // Garage // 117 m²
Private // 1999

Vrooom! is a garage in Nagoya, Japan, for an avid car enthusiast to house his collection of super cars. The challenge was to house six stunningly beautiful cars on a long narrow site, and incorporate a study and viewing area on an upper level.

Conceived as a continuous surface or road, the garage floor sweeps up to form the roof, in one gesture, framing the cars as if in a photo studio and creating a flowing aerodynamic shape.

Slender structural window mullions act as columns, supporting the roof of the garage in the same way as the roof of a car is supported, where the window frames act as the structural system. Taking the analogy further, the garage has no beams either; the profiled steel-sheet roof acts as a series of mini beams, so the garage, like a car, gets its strength from the 3D nature of steel.

The space is intentionally neutral so that attention is focused on the cars. Uplights provide an indirect source of light for the cars, avoiding any pin spots or glare from direct illumination. The final "spec" allows the garage to have its top down: the internal courtyard has a folding roof that opens up just like a cabriolet on fine days!

"A tray of rooms"

WILSON HOUSE

Chiba, Japan // Residential // 289 m² // 2008

Wilson House is a weekend house in a relaxed beachside town in Chiba, an hour and a half by train from Tokyo.

The house combines the aspirations of both client and architect: the client wanted the house to have a feeling of real solidity, and KDa was keen to open the house to its magnificent setting. In meeting these two goals, KDa drew inspiration in the wooden platform trays, called *sanbo*, found in Japan's Shinto temples. These small trays have a built-in stand, and are used in Shinto rituals to present offerings of food or other special items to the enshrined gods. KDa reinterpreted this form as a building with a solid base—two heavy walls of concrete supporting a concrete tray. Arranged on this tray is the "offering": a variety of lightweight, wooden-framed boxes.

The entry to the house is from the rear, past a separate volume containing the garage. The concrete walls of the lower level define living, kitchen and dining spaces, with the wooden structures of the upper level enclosing bedrooms and bathrooms. The entire house is directed to the river, with large windows opening to the river views and a spacious terrace for barbecues. Between the house and the river is a garden, very large by Japanese standards, which links the house with the greenery of the riverbank, where a small wooden pier allows the client to ride his jet ski to the nearby coast with his surfboard.

"Heidi goes to Sante Fe"

HEIDI HOUSE

Tokyo, Japan // Office // 158 m²
Tomohiko Matsumoto // 2005

Located in Yoyogi Uehara, a central residential area of Tokyo, Heidi House is a temporary low-cost studio and office space, completed in 2005 and built to last up to 10 years.

To help minimize costs, it was set back 3 meters from the boundary lines of neighboring sites, so no fireproofing of its external wall was necessary. This established the plan of the project but also singled out what became a popular eye-catching presence in the neighborhood.

A simple wooden frame was built and internally lined with panels of plywood for lateral strength. Careful not to compromise the integrity of the structure, alternate sections of the plywood were cut with slim baluster-shaped windows inspired by the wooden shutters artfully covering Rie Miyazawa in Kishin Shinoyama's *Sante Fe*, one of Japan's first and famous breakthrough glamour photo books. Cutouts from the windows were also used to create matching handles for the entrance's glass doors.

The wooden structure is covered in greenhouse glass. No insulation is used in the walls, leaving the plywood as a single layer. Instead, trapped air pockets between glass and wood form an economical thermal buffer. The internal sides of the plywood are painted white for an outer ring of airy studio and meeting rooms, while the building's wooden structural core, housing the business's private facilities, is wallpapered in a silky, luxuriously patterned black.

From outside, Heidi House's exposed plywood structure resembles a contemporary Swiss chalet balcony encased in glass. Its columns of unusual windows—dark by day and glowing at night—pique the curiosity. Viewed from certain angles, its plywood structure appears almost impossibly thin, yet it is this visibility of its simple construction and whimsical design that brings smiles to many passersby.

"The louvres seem to shift in color"

NAGOYA FLATS

Nagoya, Japan // Communal housing, retail // 1,580 m² // 2004

Nagoya Flats was designed on a budget to become shared residences for university students. By defying the uniform conventions of residential complexes in Japan, however, it remains an early example of a particular trend of designer apartments.

To create a dynamic façade for the ten-story building, vertical louvres of flat steel were used as balcony handrails that extend in sections to form a grid of cascading lines. Painted with a metallic polarizing coating and adjusted to different angles, the louvres seem to shift in color when viewed from different directions. During the day, they shimmer as striped blocks of silvery blues and grays. By nightfall, their silhouettes almost disappear ahead of the glowing, horizontal strips of the lit apartments.

Inside, exposed concrete ceilings are matched with wooden flooring and minimalist white or engineered wood walls and fittings. Open staircases allow light from balconies to reach all corners. Kitchenettes are hidden behind sliding doors that double as striking accent walls. The use of bold colors and textures for contrasting feature walls or fittings ensures that each apartment is unique.

"Panoramic views of the sea and coastline"

M HOUSE

Shimoda, Japan // Residential // 275 m²
Private // 2001

M House sits 20 meters above Iritahama Beach in Izu, which has been voted Japan's best beach for several years in a row. A heavily wooded hill forms the backdrop to the house, commanding a dramatic 270-degree panoramic view of the sea and coastline.

The national park location dictated a pitched roof. The house uses the full width of the long and narrow site along a steep slope, so it had to be cantilevered out over the steeply falling land—quite a challenge on a sand bluff!

Strong typhoons regularly hit this area of Japan, and although there was a desire for the windows facing the ocean to be completely glazed, there was a very practical need to protect it from strong winds, wind-blown debris being the main danger. Rather than toughening the glass, which is costly, fibreglass floor gratings were used as debris screens. The sliding screens also act as sun shading and privacy screens, and help contain the space within the house, preventing it from feeling too open.

"The largest timber retail building in Japan"

G-BUILDING

Tokyo, Japan // Retail // 903 m²
Japan Retail Fund Investment // 2016

The G-Building, an environmentally conscious landmark within the genteel Tokyo neighborhood of Jiyugaoka, is defined by the beauty and versatility of wood. When completed in 2016, it was the largest timber retail building in Japan.

Inspired by the residential nature of Jiyugaoka, the thick timber walls of the G-Building exterior transition into a pitched roof to delineate a silhouette of a house. Its glass façade, a bold *amidakuji* ladder pattern of windows, is inset at a gentle angle to reveal a triangular slice of the structure's wooden soffit and wall, and draw the eye of approaching passersby to the interiors.

Inside and out, details are key to the contemporary use of the time-honored architectural material. The texture, grain and warm hues of cross-laminated timber create a sense of lightness that belie the density and dimensions of the building's exposed beams, columns and walls. The structure perceptually melts away, its wooden elements becoming elegant design features of generous retail spaces. Tenants need only to bring display units and furniture, making changes in residency efficient and economical, and reducing interior refurbishing waste.

Designed for a property developer, the G-Building, built with timber engineered by Shelter, a Japanese FSC-certified manufacturer, also sets a precedent for sustainable and adaptable commercial structures. The original tenant required open-plan floor spaces, but in anticipation of the building's future as a home to several boutiques, each floor was designed with two entrances. This allowed each one to be split into two independent units.

The structure's core, a roomy stairwell that winds around a hidden elevator shaft, connects all four floors both physically and visually. Wrapped in glass, it offers visitors sweeping views of surrounding retail spaces and glimpses of the neighborhood beyond their windows. A spacious, decked roof terrace completes the building's airy ambience, connecting its natural structure to the outdoors.

KOE
KOE

"What we need is a big straw hat"

HOME-FOR-ALL FOR CHILDREN

Soma, Japan // Children's play space // 1,552 m²
Soma City // 2015

KDa's Home-for-All project in Soma City, Japan, was handed over to the local community on February 14, 2015, with much love.

The Home-for-All initiative was set up within months of the 2011 Tohoku earthquake and tsunami, to build small community centers in the heart of the acres of temporary housing that were built to replace the 250,000 homes that were destroyed.

To date, thanks to incredibly generous donations from Japan and all around the world, sixteen Home-for-All buildings have been built.

Conceived as a large straw hat held aloft by trees, this building is an indoor play space for children up to the age of four. These spaces are important due to the ongoing concerns about background radiation levels. As the children cannot play outside, the building was designed to feel like the children are playing in a park with trees. The cross-laminated timber columns help reduce the span of the timber roof, making it lighter, and have been designed to resemble trees, complete with their own wildlife!

The roof is made up of nine layers of timber slats. Each slat is continuous, the longest being 20 meters. The slats are laid over a formwork one layer at a time, with each successive layer rotated 120 degrees.

The project was made possible by donations from all over Japan through the T-Point card system and the generous in-kind support by many construction material and equipment suppliers. All professional services for the project were provided pro bono.

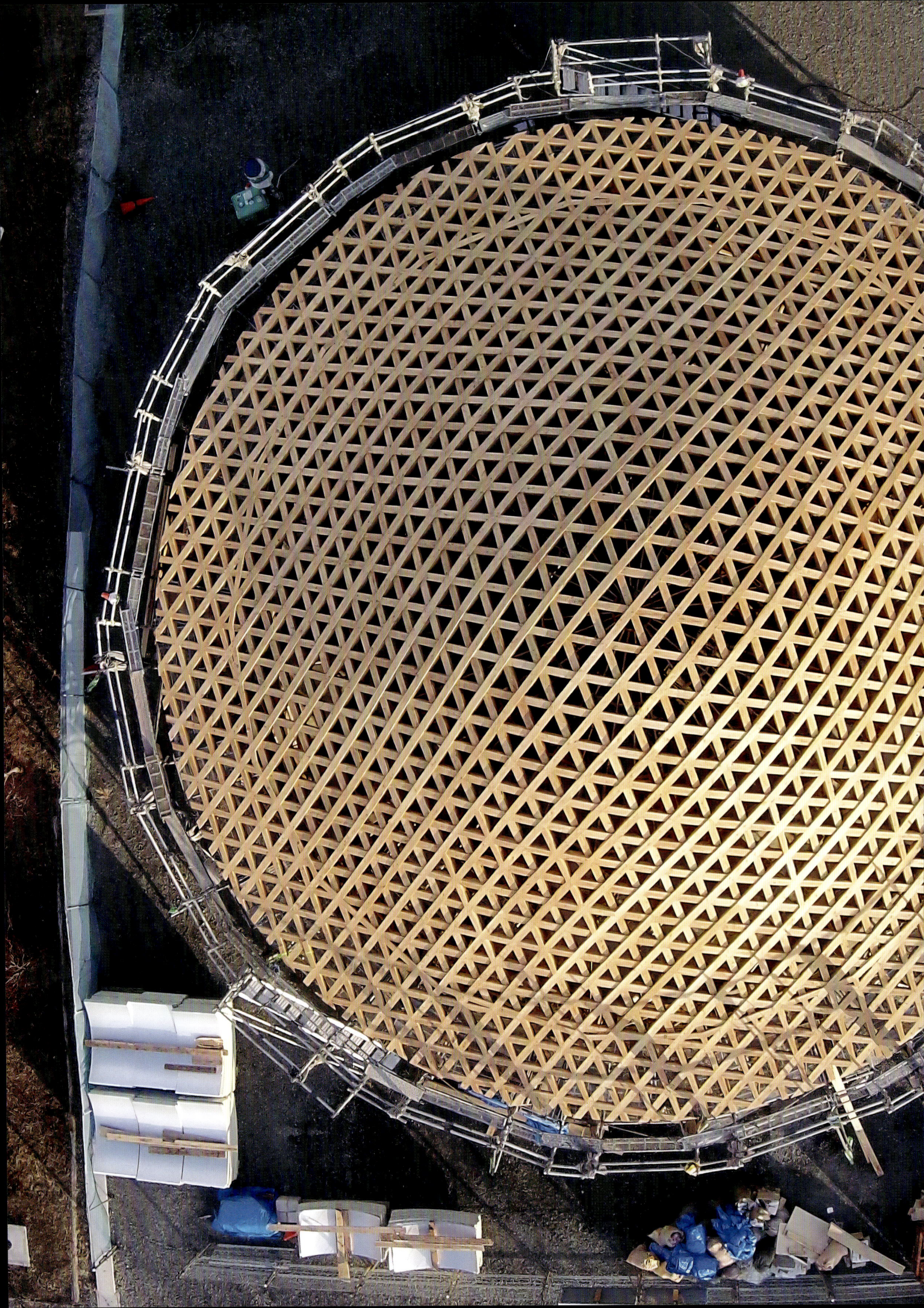

vitra.

Jichin-sai

No matter what kind of building you enter in Japan—whether it's a modest shrine or a towering office skyscraper—it's likely that you are stepping onto blessed land.

The *jichin-sai* groundbreaking ceremony is a celebratory ritual of architectural and civil engineering projects. A social custom rooted in mythology and Shintoism, it's performed by Shinto priests who call upon local deities, known as *kami*, to purify and bless land for safe construction.

A ceremonial enclosure is prepared on the barren land of a building site. Leafy stalks of bamboo are erected in each corner of the space and tied to one another by sacred straw rope hung with paper streamers. Inside the enclosure stands a wooden, eight-legged altar laden with offerings displayed around the *himorogi*, a branch of the sakaki tree (Cleyera Japonica) that serves as a vessel to enshrine the local *kami*.

The enticing bounty of offerings often catches the eye. Most times it's an array of simple farm produce or local foods—bright carrots, cabbages, shiny eggplants, giant tomatoes, colorful apples, oranges and bananas, perhaps a golden pineapple, or even a freshly caught fish. Other times, the gifts are simply supermarket snacks, such as bags of rice crackers or packets of mochi cakes and bottles of sake.

Before the ceremony begins, participants—usually the project's architect, property owner and chief construction foreman—take part in a purifying handwashing ritual. The priest then invokes the *kami*, inviting it to the *himorogi* and offerings, and recites a *norito* incantation, his rhythmic chant beseeching the deity to oversee the safe development of land. A *shiho-harai* purification ritual of the grounds follows. Here, salt, sake, rice, or confetti-like squares of paper are tossed across the four corners of the enclosure.

Three symbolic rites performed as an appeasement ritual become a highlight of *jichin-sai: karisome* grass cutting, *ugachisome* ground leveling and *kuwaire*, the breaking of ground. The architect is given a wooden sickle to cut down blades of grass planted atop a mound of earth. Next, the property owner smooths the mound with a wooden hoe, before the chief construction foreman digs through it with a spade. For some *jichin-sai*, the *kuwaire* involves the burial of *shizumemono*, a paulownia box of tiny metal silhouettes of samurai swords, a shield, a spear, a mirror, a jade ball, and a human figure. The box of talismans is often re-buried later within the foundations of the new building.

Finally, each participant approaches the altar to place offerings of *tamagushi*, sacred sprigs of the sakaki tree, before the priest performs a closing ritual releasing the *kami* to ascend back to nature.

"Always here to help"

KOBAN

Kumamoto, Japan // Police station // 144 m²
Kumamoto Prefectural Police Headquarters // 2011

This project forms part of the celebrated Kumamoto Artpolis program. The program, designed to provide Kumamoto, a center of the southernmost island of Japan, with world-class public buildings, has resulted in masterpieces by Japanese stars such as Toyo Ito, Kazuyo Sejima, Tadao Ando, and Kazuo Shinohara.

KDa's *koban*, or neighborhood police station, is located near Kumamoto's new railway station and was required to stand out as a local landmark but present a friendly image. To make the requested sculptural gesture, KDa wrapped the top of the building in a ribbon of perforated steel plate and colored the upper floor space and the inside of the ribbon with a gentle rainbow gradation. This bold graphic can be seen from all around the neighborhood, but up close it creates subtle effects by casting shadows on the surrounding road. While the ribbon was not part of the brief for the building, KDa have cunningly made it functional: a 3-meter cantilever creates a shelter where patrol cars can park, allowing the police to enter and exit without getting wet. The whole building mirrors the police car's horizontal color stratification—complete with a red light!

KOBAN
THE KUMAMOTO TOWER
POLICE

KOBAN

KOBAN
KOBAN
POLICE

"A bamboo grove in the city"

BILLBOARD BUILDING

Tokyo, Japan // Retail // 37 m²
Risa Partners // 2005

Tokyo is filled with tiny buildings on awkward sites—what fellow Tokyo-based architect Yoshiharu Tsukamoto has called "pet architecture."

These are wedged onto tiny slivers of land left over from the slicing and dicing of land through processes of urban planning and property development. While small and unassuming, they are often charming, even lovable, like wildflowers growing between cracks in the hard surfaces of the city. This building is KDa's response to this phenomenon—their very own pet architecture.

The building is tiny. It is an 11-meter-long, two-story high wedge, 2.5 meters wide at one end and tapering to just 600 millimeters at the other. Although small, it has a prominent position facing a well-trafficked road. The building, now serving as a jeweler's workspace and shop, was built on spec. With a function that was initially vague, but being nearly all front, KDa's "pet" became what it so obviously wanted to be: an inhabitable billboard.

With this decision, the severe constraints of the project suddenly blossomed into a multiplicity of possibilities. With a billboard for a building, the façade becomes image, and image becomes façade. Working up the main elevation becomes an exercise in photo editing and graphic manipulation. The choice of image was crucial. Green has long given way to gray in central Tokyo. Why not use this opportunity to offer a gentle reminder of what once flourished in the cool valleys of Azabu?

KDa used a strong, simple image of a bamboo grove, abstracted and stenciled in white, on the glass façade, with the back wall bright green. In architectural terms, this treatment subtly modulates the transition from opacity to transparency across the width of the billboard façade.

By day, it also offers a simple and effective form of sun-shading. But by night, when its reflected green light dapples over the intersection, it offers the casual passerby something rather magical: a vision of a luminous bamboo plantation in the heart of the metropolis.

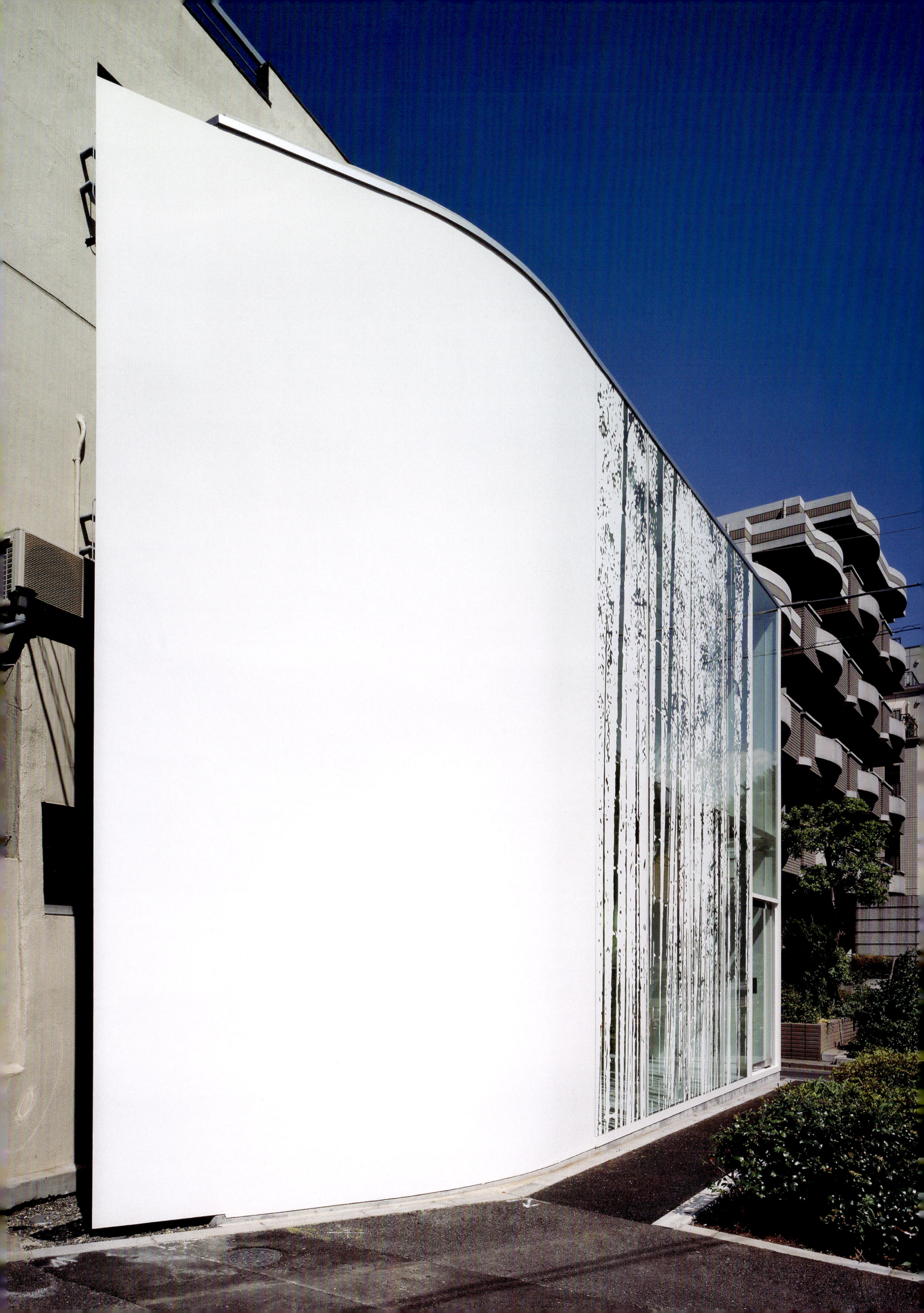

ATM

ATM

Good Design賞
なにか いいことが ありますように
FATHER OF TAKENOKO

"A pearl in a shell"

IDÉE WORKSTATION

Tokyo, Japan // Showroom // 193 m²
IDÉE // 1996

Idée Workstation, KDa's first architectural project, was ahead of its time in Japan. A furniture firm's headquarters structured around the renovation of a former petrol station kiosk, it challenged a national mindset of razing properties. The client, Teruo Kurosaki, was renowned for embracing the unusual. His Idée furniture introduced Japan to the now-iconic organic forms and bold colors of Marc Newson and other trailblazing designers.

For Kurosaki, the simple concrete kiosk evoked the resilience of postwar Japan. As the core of a three-story flagship store, the kiosk stands within two levels of showrooms and below a third-floor atelier. Like a golden pearl in a shell, it remains its own entity as private offices, painted vibrant yellow and surrounded by capacious showroom spaces. A framework of white, industrial-inspired steel interiors opens up the showrooms further. The transparency of its expanded metal section of second-story flooring and staircase emphasizes the kiosk, while enhancing the visual depth and vertical flow of space. Daylight from the west-facing wall of windows bounces off every surface to create a bright, airy and neutral backdrop to Idée's striking, pop-colored furniture.

Pink, blue, yellow, and orange film covering panels of the second-floor windows reflect the Idée aesthetic, their sunlit hues casting shadows across the white interiors like stained glass. The flooring is coated in a glossy epoxy resin, which accentuates the luminous effect as the colorful shadows shift and change with daylight. On the first floor, an unusual accent wall introduces a new architectural material: designer Jane Atfield's pioneering "made of waste" plastic panels. Derived from discarded bottles, it was among the first recycled plastic industrial design materials.

Outside, a translucent polycarbonate veil billows over two-thirds of the glass façade, its futuristic, fluid shape drawing attention as it gently leans over the sidewalk. From within, the veil softens light and offers privacy in the atelier and second-floor showroom.

Idée Workstation transforms as the sun sets. By day, the sweeping curve of its veil draws the eye to the first-floor stars of the building: Idée's vivid and unique chairs and tables. At night, lit from inside, the entire structure becomes a translucent luminous grid of color—a beacon of pioneering design in Japan.

idée
WORK
sta+
-ION

"Its pixelated pink orchid pattern creates an internal world"

R3 UKISHIMA / AI CAFÉ 54

Naha, Japan // Retail, café spaces // 492 m²
Risa Partners // 2007

Ai Café, a four-unit commercial building, is located just off Kokusai Dori, the main tourist street in Naha, capital of Okinawa. It is here in Ukishima Dori that many trendy boutiques and galleries are located; here is where Okinwawa's tradition and young culture meet.

The site presented a major challenge: a long street frontage facing the side of a bland convenience store onto which all four retail units had to face, including the café. The response became the key element of the building: a 25-meter-long, 5-meter-high perforated concrete block screen that encloses a balcony access to the second floor while screening off the convenience store, and electricity and telephone wires running along the street. The screen with its pixelated pink orchid pattern creates an internal world for the café while letting air and light into the building.

A four-story tower at one end of the building allows it to be seen from Kokusai Dori, giving it a strong presence on the main road, while the low perforated concrete block screen gives the project a more comfortable scale on the narrower Ukishima street.

オリジナル
ストラップ製作

"A 20-meter hanger rail please"

UNDERCOVER LAB

Tokyo, Japan // Retail // 638 m²
Undercover Lab // 2001

Tucked away in the backstreets of Tokyo's fashion mecca of Harajuku, Undercover Lab houses the studio, press showroom, staff atelier, and warehouse of its eponymous avant-garde designer label.

Built on a flag-shaped plot of land, Undercover Lab is "undercover" itself, hidden behind an inconspicuous building and connected to the street by a long, narrow driveway. Its anonymity adds to the enigmatic nature of a cantilevered black box that mysteriously protrudes 10 meters over the driveway like a levitating shipping container.

The cantilever structure is both a design feature and an architectural solution. It extends Undercover Lab's 10-meter-square main building to accommodate a 20-meter-long clothing rail, a requirement of the fashion house's press room. Attached to the second floor of the main building, its rooftop also provides an unusual open-air catwalk.

A simple staircase of expanded metal separates the press room from the main building, allowing Undercover to keep its creative affairs away from prying eyes. On the opposite side of the building, a continuous sloping glass wall allows daylight to illuminate the top-floor atelier and the meeting room below. Only the warehouse on the first floor is enclosed to protect its contents. In the basement lies the studio, a covert and private space, still lit by daylight from the window wall via an opening above.

Undercover designer Jun Takahashi's rebellious personality and love of British punk influence the building's aesthetics. As if to defy the established trend of exposed-concrete architecture, the untreated wooden formwork, which is usually removed once concrete is set, is kept in place on the studio ceiling and stairwell walls. Recycled gymnasium wooden floorboards instill a raw warmth to the interiors, and weather-worn London yellow stock bricks create accent walls and the Undercover Lab's unconventional façade.

"Ultra super-luxury"

VERTU

Tokyo, Japan // Flagship retail // 230 m²
Vertu // 2008

Vertu is a British-based manufacturer of luxury mobile phones. Designing a new Tokyo boutique in elegant Ginza in which to present such exquisitely crafted objects, KDa sought to create an interior that matched the sophistication and attention-to-detail of the phones. The black-and-white interior of the ground-floor display area uses a palette of high-quality materials, such as high-gloss urethane lacquer and glass display cases tinted using techniques normally employed in luxury cars. In the stairs to the second floor, the custom-designed balustrade is made of stainless-steel mesh embossed with Vertu logos and sandwiched in glass. The second floor accommodates a VIP area—reflecting its exclusive character, the room includes red lacquer panels and a hand-tufted red carpet.

VERTU
VERTU
VERTU

"Listen and believe"

KEF MUSIC GALLERY

Tokyo, Japan // Retail, gallery // 202 m²
KEF // 2023

The KEF Music Gallery, located in Aoyama, a stylish design district of Tokyo, is a two-story experiential space in which to explore the creative world of KEF high-fidelity sound. Instantly recognizable from afar, its glass façade features a huge 3D graphic interpretation of KEF's signature Uni-Q driver array. The iconic design transforms the building into a giant, illuminated, transparent speaker. Like a beacon, it draws visitors into two floors of experiential showrooms and three split-floor levels of sound rooms.

More than a showroom or store, its spaces are multifaceted, designed to be lively hubs of creative social activity. Visitors are encouraged to try innovative speaker and headphone designs and experience the sound quality of KEF's architectural loudspeakers. Collaborators—local artists, designers, musicians and sound producers—are invited to use KEF equipment to showcase works.

Both the ground-floor Gallery and first-floor Studio feature sound absorption walls fitted with adjustable floating shelves to allow for flexible and ever-changing displays of KEF's wireless active speakers. Full-height glazed windows are also fitted with moveable LED monitors to showcase digital installations, videos and original collaborative works.

A stair tower of shelving for KEF's greatest and latest products extends through the floors to become the heart of the structure—a centerpiece that guides visitors from the Gallery and Studio to three split-floor rooms of immersive sound experiences.

On the lower-ground level, the Ultimate Experience Room interior is fine-tuned by sound engineers to create the optimum soundscape for Ross Lovegrove's first design for KEF—a pair of futuristic, 2-meter-tall MUON speakers. Above, the Wireless High-Fidelity Lounge, a comfy living room space, demonstrates the sound quality and range of KEF's LS60 wireless speakers. The uppermost level, the Extreme Theatre, provides an intimate home cinema experience of ultimate surround sound, featuring eight sets of reference speakers installed in walls, behind the screen and in the ceiling.

As a combined retail and exhibition space, KEF Music Gallery not only presents KEF's full range of high-fidelity speaker technology, but is also an interactive platform to explore its potential with cutting-edge partners.

KEF Music Gallery
TOKYO

Precision Parking

One of the many joys of living and working in Japan is experiencing the country's remarkable precision. From the famous, down-to-the-second punctuality of its trains to pop concerts that start exactly on time, Japan thrives on accuracy and attention to detail. Construction sites are no exception to this rule. A memorable example is the pre-opening tour of Fumihiko Maki's Tepia building in Tokyo. During the event, architects in attendance were handed small rulers—and even magnifying glasses—to meticulously inspect the building's intricate details. This speaks to Japan's unwavering commitment to precision in all aspects of life.

This national obsession with detail extends beyond architecture and public transportation, right down to something as seemingly mundane as parking a car. In fact, parking in Japan has become an art form, driven by the necessity of maximizing space. Given the country's limited land area, residential plots tend to be small, and as a result, so are the garages. For homeowners and drivers, this means parking can be a real challenge, requiring exceptional skill and care to navigate tight spaces.

KDa has become fascinated with this phenomenon, and over the years, has collected a series of photographs capturing this "precision parking." These images showcase everything from cars squeezed perfectly into garages that seem barely big enough, to vehicles aligned so exactly with the boundaries of a space that not an inch is wasted. What might appear to be an everyday task becomes a display of the same meticulousness that governs the country's architecture, infrastructure and public life.

In Japan, precision parking is not just a necessity, it's a reflection of a broader cultural value. Whether it's a small family car tucked neatly between two buildings or a luxury sedan parked within millimeters of its garage walls, the care taken in parking illustrates a deep respect for order and efficiency. This level of precision extends into the most routine aspects of life, adding a layer of elegance to something as simple as pulling into a parking spot.

For those who have had the pleasure of living and working in Japan, this everyday perfection is a constant source of delight and admiration.

"Bringing fun back to bath time!"

GUMI BATH

Milan, Italy // Installation // 5 m²
Interni Magazine // 2002

As part of the illustrious Milano Salone, KDa was invited by *Interni Magazine* to participate in "Interni in Piazza," a two-week installation of "rooms" in the main piazzas of Milan. Seven architects participated, including KDa. Each architect was teamed up with an Italian material sponsor. KDa chose Technogel, a memory gel used in wheelchair seats and for surgical pillows, and also chose to put the most private room, the bathroom, in the most public space: a piazza.

Bathrooms have traditionally been made of hard, slippery, and cold materials and can be quite dangerous. With new materials such as Technogel, KDa decided that the bathroom can be soft, non-slippery and warm to the touch.

The freestanding bathroom comprises a hand basin, bath and shower. The structure is a blue-tinted, 20-millimeter-thick acrylic ribbon made by Waazwiz. Soft tiles were then bonded to the acrylic. The tiles are a watery translucent blue with a 3D duck molded into the tile, playing ironically with the old image of hard ceramic bathroom tiles, bringing fun back to bath time!

"Your flexible friend"

DORADORA

Furniture // Karimoku // 2017

Manufactured by Karimoku, one of Japan's largest woodworking companies, doradora was launched in 2017, just as shifts in employee work-life priorities began to evolve in Japan. Offices were becoming more inviting, coworking spaces commonplace, and remote working increasingly popular.

Modular, customizable, and playful, doradora is a flexible furniture solution, designed to suit and enhance any such environment or situation. Its gentle curved forms, natural wood tones, and colorful textiles evoke the warm and welcoming ambience of home, whether in an office, lobby, café, or lounge.

The modular seat design allows for multiple uses: independent chairs, benches, day beds, or long curvy sofas that encourage face-to-face interaction with coworkers, friends, or family. Wooden legs at the sides of each seat base can be extended upward with a series of detachable, functional accessories. Slot on a lamp for a reading nook, add a side table for working, or create a comfy couch with backrests. Other options include a coat stand, a planter and even a champagne bucket for office celebrations and parties. Seat fabrics, too, can be custom-ordered to complement existing décor, while the wooden accessories can be printed with matching graphic patterns.

With so many seating and accessory configurations, doradora can keep changing, constantly adapting to its space and needs.

"A kaleidoscopic array of velvet, vinyl, leather, and satin"

KUNE-KUNE BENCH

Nagaoka, Japan // Furniture
Nagaoka City // 1996

KDa was invited to design seating elements for the huge foyer space of a new theater complex, Nagaoka Lyric Hall, designed by architect Toyo Ito. Contained within the building are a concert hall and two theaters, all of which serve different audiences at different times. Unrestricted by the partitions that commonly fill up public spaces of this kind, KDa designed benches that meander snake-like through the lobby. Replacing the ubiquitous but unsightly pole partitions they can, if needed, serve as partitions by pulling a belt out of one bench end and connecting it to the next one. Finished in a kaleidoscopic array of velvet, vinyl, leather, and satin materials in matching colors, the swirling snake shapes leave a lasting impression of a fun foyer.

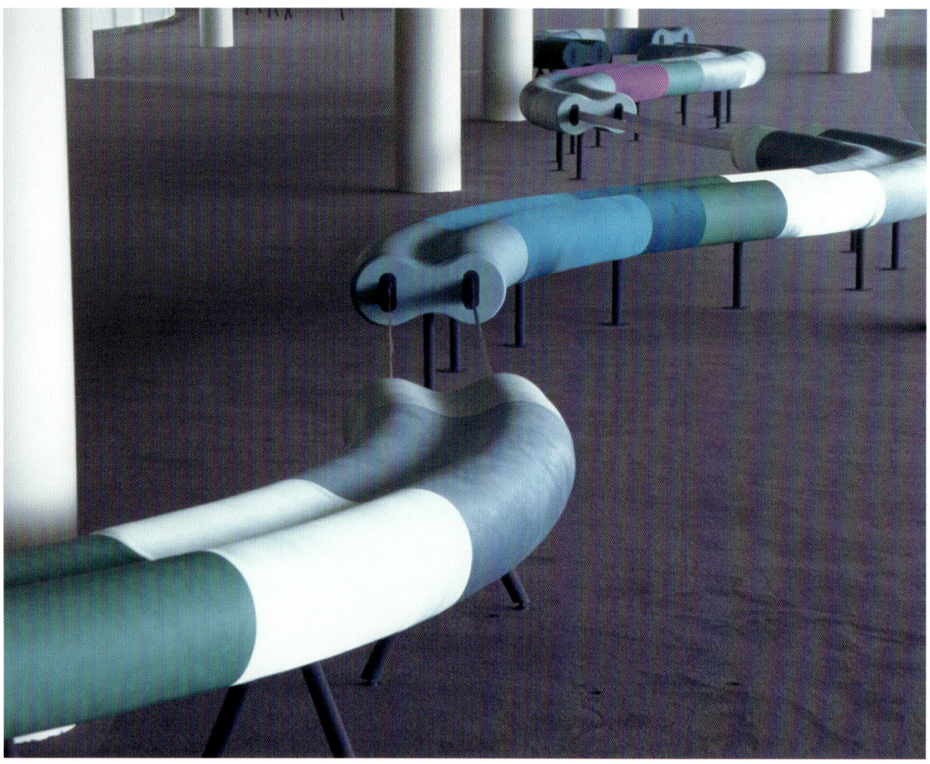

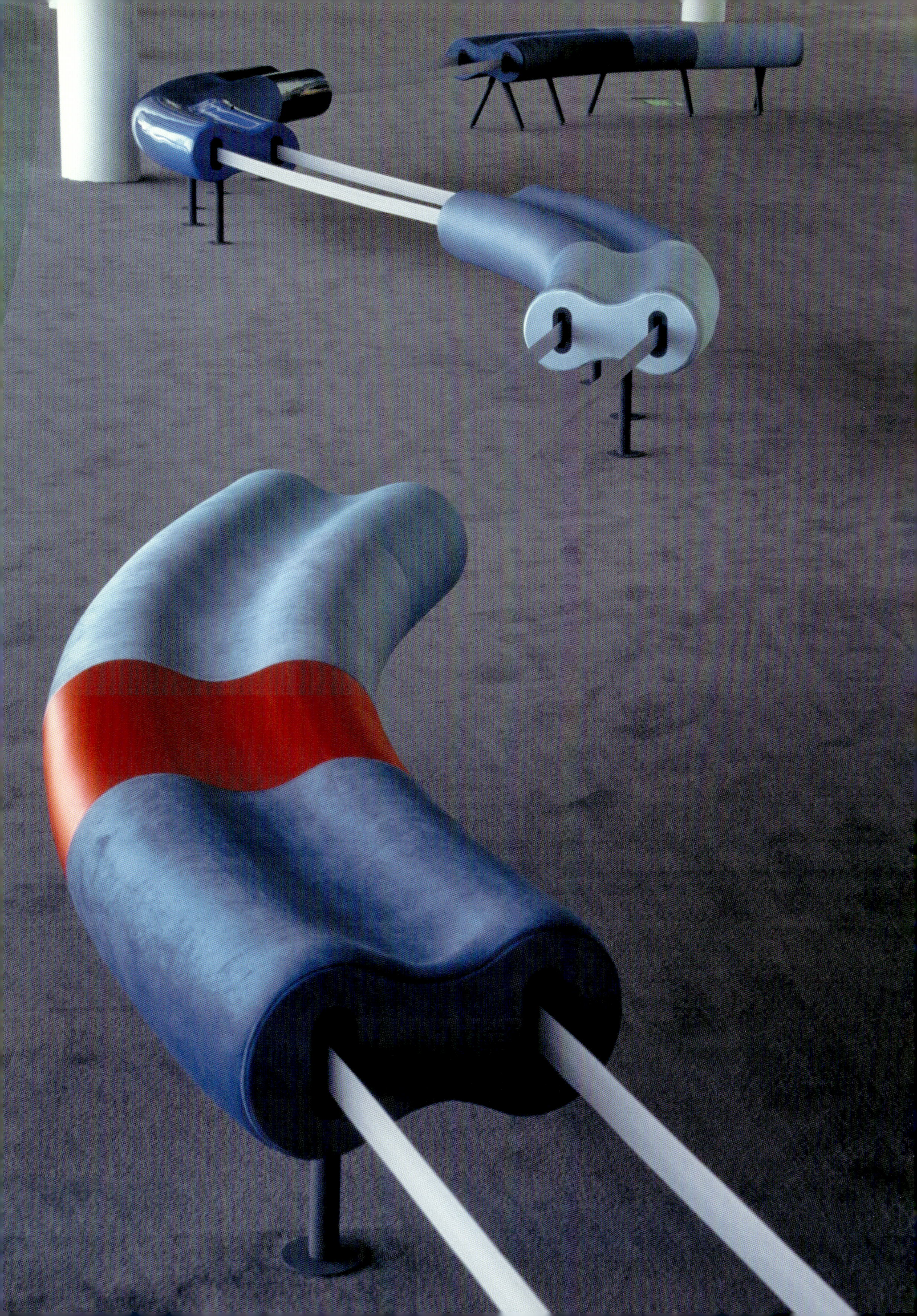

"Sparkling display of trees"

LAFORET HARAJUKU RIN RIN

Tokyo, Japan // Streetscape // 819 m²
Mori Building // 2001

The Laforet department store has long been the primary destination for young fashion in Tokyo. Laforet was looking to enter the new century with a bright, new, fresh image to match.

To unify and strengthen the presence of the 50-meter store frontage, KDa designed a row of stainless-steel "window case" trees that, when seen from the pavement at a shallow angle, appear almost as a continuous wall, but when seen directly, appear as a series of gateways into the store.

The beautiful plane trees lining the front of Laforet were cut down as the design process was happening, due to the construction of a new subway line. The tree motif was inspired by the memory of the lost plane trees and also by the department store's French name, Laforet, derived originally from the owner's name, Mori, Japanese for forest. The word consists of three tree kanji characters. KDa added another tree kanji and came up with a new word, *rin rin*, meaning "little woods."

年中無休
カラオケ&バー
P

"There's never enough green in a city"

GREEN GREEN SCREEN

Tokyo, Japan // Construction fence // 1,080 m²
Mori Building // 2003

This live and growing construction screen, 274 meters long, ran almost the full length of Tokyo's version of the Champs-Élysées, Omotesando. The screen was there for 3 years while Tadao Ando's large mixed-use development was under construction behind it. The idea was a wall that would show the passage of time; something that would grow and mature over 3 years.

The Doujunkai apartment buildings were known for their endearing greenery and KDa felt this nature should be added back into the city for the duration of the construction. Thirteen different types of evergreen ivy, plants, and grass were chosen to grow from felt pockets attached to the screen.

Similar to a barcode, the different greens formed a pattern of stripes along the entire length. A variety of graphic wallpaper patterns, again on the theme of leaves and plants in a green palette, were interspersed among the real greens. Yet more stripes of varying width were covered by high-end advertising.

There is never enough green in a city. Construction sites are noisy, dirty, and dusty, so KDa wanted to create the antidote to it: a reminder of nature with bird-chirping sounds and cool mist emanating from the leafy wall.

"World-famous, award-winning construction fence"

PIKA PIKA PRETZEL

Tokyo, Japan // Construction fence // 680 m²
VELOQX // 1999

Pika Pika Pretzel was an early KDa project that re-imagined a construction fence into a playful 3D installation. The brief was to create an eye-catching, illuminated and demountable hoarding. It had to be head-turning—a breathtaking monument to indicate that the construction behind was about to become the most exciting hot spot in Harajuku.

Silver inflatables were installed above the hoarding to soar like floating bouquets of balloons. Each inflatable comprised seven different-sized puffed-up rings that allowed the structure to withstand gusts of wind and formed petite windows to offer alluring glimpses of the site behind. The inner sides of the rings were translucent to allow a gleam of light to emanate from within.

At 34 meters wide and 20 meters tall, the structure glistened by day and glowed at night like a dramatic pop art installation. The silver rings seemed to drift upward from clusters of purple circles of the hoarding below, looking like gigantic sparkling pretzels. Hence its whimsical name.

34m
WIDE
HAPPY
ARAJUKU'S
RIGHTEST
カピカ
SPOT

"Inflate for fun"

UK98 PAVILION

Locations across Japan // Demountable pavilion // 60 m² each
British Embassy Tokyo // 1998

Designed for UK98, a year-long festival of British culture in Japan, this demountable and flexible pavilion was built using cutting-edge technologies from the UK such as those developed by high-tech yacht-mast-maker Proctor Masts and leading hot-air-balloon manufacturer Cameron Balloons.

Based on a system of interlocking circles, similar to traditional Japanese trays, this allowed the five elements to be arranged in a straight line, radial pattern, and curve, or as individual units.

Each of the five elements was packed into four curved crates that formed the seating when unpacked and could be filled with water bladders to secure the pavilion in position when windy.

MG
LAND ROVER
Virgin
Virgin
virgin

Virgin
Virgin

Virgin
Virgin

ROVER

"Walk this way"

GALLERY MA

Tokyo, Japan // Exhibition // TOTO // 2009

The key to KDa's design for the exhibition was their fascination with materials, objects and ideas around them in Tokyo that were often invisible to people who live in Japan.

The exhibition occupied Gallery MA's two floors and courtyard. The lower gallery was filled with the mobile *kanban* signs found in the streets outside of most of Tokyo's bars. Topped with flashing lights and a big "this way" arrow, the signs displayed backlit photographs of KDa's projects. These signs were also used in the courtyard.

Instead of classic 3D architectural models, KDa used a new 3D-printing technique used by the makers of inexpensive crystal souvenirs. KDa took the largest crystal blocks that the manufacturer could deal with and had twenty of their projects modeled using the technique. The laser-produced models display incredible detail and have a remarkable visual quality: when viewed from the side the models reveal perfect elevations; viewed from above they reveal the plan; and from any other angle they present X-ray views of and through whole buildings. Displayed in a black painted room, the models were lit from below, each displayed on a slowly rotating turntable.

SonyMusic

"The secret life of toilets"

GALLERY TOTO

Narita, Japan // Public toilet // 138 m²
TOTO // 2015

Gallery TOTO in the newly built Sky Lounge "WA" of Narita International Airport Terminal 2 doubled as a showroom for the iconic brand's state-of-the art designs while providing an essential facility for the modern traveler.

Intrigued by the notion of the most private place simultaneously being in a very public place, KDa conceived the Gallery as a clear glass box with four toilets each for men and women, a fully accessible universal toilet, and a nursing room for parents—all randomly placed. The Gallery features a host of the latest digital technology including a fabric-like façade screen containing low-resolution LED panels that transform each toilet exterior wall facing the public lounge space into a digital screen. A series of funny, moving silhouetted images by contemporary dance company Strange Kinoko suggest that dance parties to cleaning sequences are happening inside the toilet spaces.

Unlike traditional closed public toilets, this gave the whole space a kind of intriguing openness, which made curious visitors wander in, even if they needn't necessarily use the facilities—the perfect showroom.

GALLERY TOTO

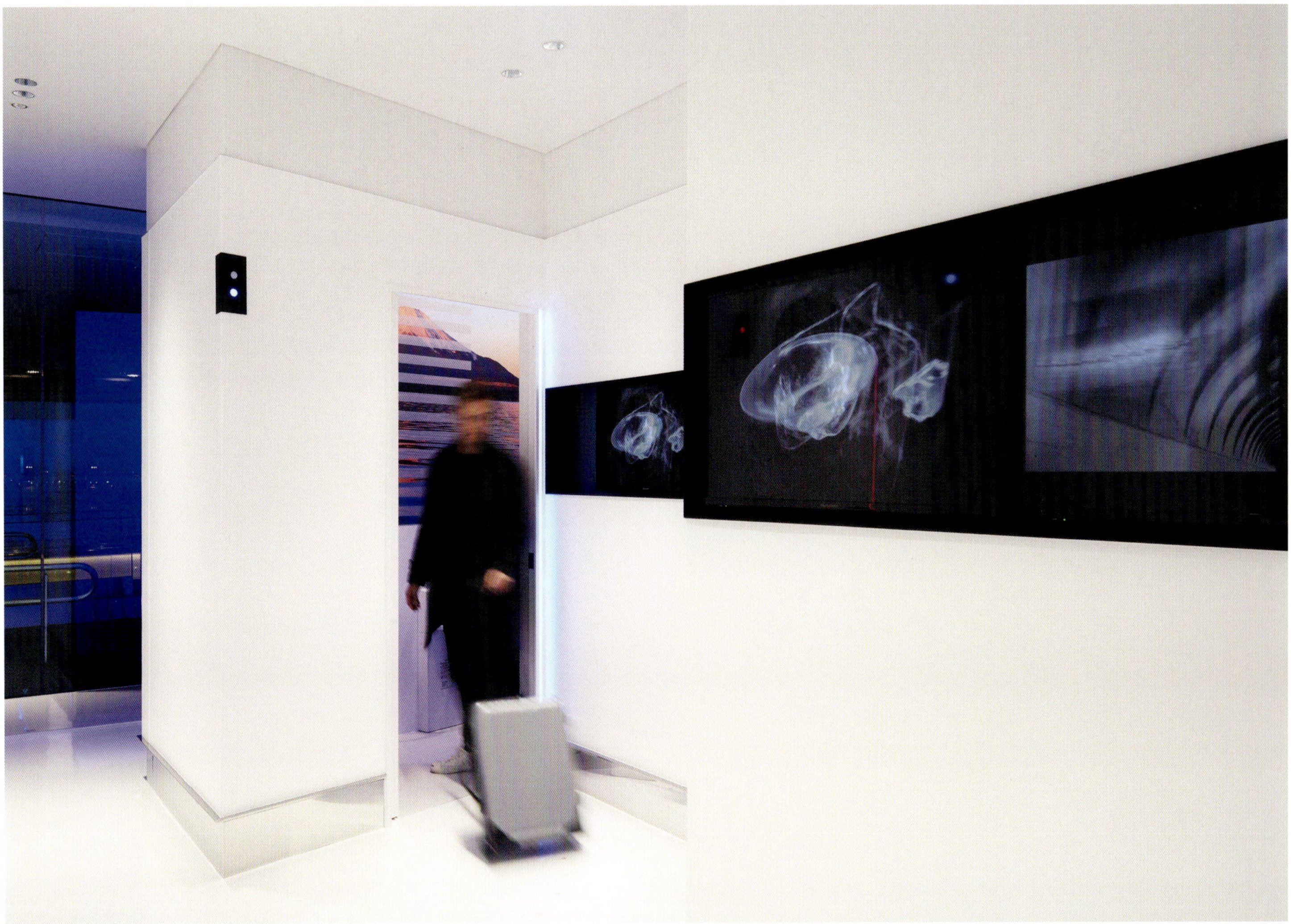

"Demystifying data screens"

BLOOMBERG ICE

Tokyo, Japan // Office lobby installation // 5 x 3.5 m
Bloomberg // 2002

Bloomberg is about communication and information. This had to be conveyed in a way that would appeal to all age groups, in this very public space opposite Tokyo Station in the heart of Marunouchi.

In the very early stages of the project, KDa invited Toshio Iwai to collaborate on this project. Iwai was one of the world's leading artists in interface design with a knack for demystifying computers and data.

An icicle-like pure white element in the space allowed clouds of information to condense. In its resting mode with no one interacting with it, stock tickers were expressed in a fun and easily understandable way. If the stock was up, the ticker fonts would swell; if it fell, they shrank and dropped below the line.

As visitors approached ICE, the infrared sensors behind the glass wall detected their presence and they began to interact with the data. A range of games like a huge digital harp or an interactive volleyball game added to the fun, and ICE became the biggest touchscreen art installation of its time.

New Year Cards

New Year is the most important holiday in Japan. Businesses close for several days, family gatherings take priority, traditional feasts are prepared, and shrines are visited. For Japan Post, however, it's the busiest time of the year as its sorting offices overflow with thousands upon thousands of *nengajo* New Year's cards—all to be dutifully delivered on January 1.

Nengajo usually feature the New Year's zodiac animal and are sent to relatives, friends, clients, acquaintances, and anyone of importance to the sender. It is a tradition that dates back to the Heian Period (794–1185), and it can take hours to days to compile *nengajo* lists and prepare each one. Yet, even today, many still find the time to illustrate and write them by hand.

To KDa, sending *nengajo* is an inspiring custom. It's a creative way to offer others a token of appreciation, wish them a prosperous new year, and spread a little joy. For over 30 years, KDa has delighted in designing KDa *nengajo*, experimenting with the postcard format, playing with imagery and parody, and indulging in a little humor.

KDa turns each one into a small thank-you gift of pop art, often attaching everyday objects as playful graphic elements: candy, bath salts, plastic spoons, condiment sachets, even dog biscuits.

In 2000, a "Y2K compliant" air-activated hand-warmer sachet was taped to the card with the guarantee of being "bug proof." In 2005, the year of the rooster, a red-and-white Colonel Sanders-like Mark Dytham appeared on the card, while Astrid Klein featured on the wrapper of an attached wet-wipe sachet. Inspired by PANTONE® colors in 2008, the year of the mouse, the *nengajo* became a rodent-nibbled swatch of six species of mouse, each representing a different "KDaTONE®" gray.

Every design brought about a year-end, enthusiastic labour of love. The miniature nunchucks attached to the kitsch 2012 film poster of Mark performing a Bruce Lee-style flying kick, for the year of the dragon, had to be individually constructed from thousands of tiny pieces of plastic and chain. For 2013, the year of the snake, a luminous pink "snake oil" was concocted and pipetted into 1,000 miniature vials. Finding the perfect sheep for a 2015 photoshoot comically involved selecting a beauty from the farm equivalent of a model agency portfolio.

Only once has there been a hiccup with the KDa *nengajo*. In an incident, perhaps less amusing for Japan Post than it was for KDa, they discovered that ketchup sachets can explode dramatically during the mailing process.

Nothing, however, deters KDa from continuing to enjoy pushing the envelope on *nengajo* cards.

A HAPPY CHRISTMAS AND A WARM MILLENNIUM ARE GUARANTEED WITH THIS BUG PROOF HAND WARMER
ホカロンミニ
Klein Dytham architecture wishes you a happy new year
count them over the fence for sweet dreams in the year of the sheep 2003
2004 - Let's go bananas in the year of the monkey !
KDa
we're not CHICKEN in the year of the ROOSTER !!!
KLEIN DYTHAM
THEY'RE GR-R-REAT!
TONY
Klein Dytham architecture
wishes you a magical Year of the Rabbit !!
KLEIN DYTHAM ARCHITECTURE WISHES YOU A FRESH START TO 2007!!!
WET IN
KDaTONE
Go gray in the year of the mouse!
KLEIN DYTHAM ARCHITECTURE
Klein Dytham architecture
wish you a BULLISH
2009
in the year of the Ox!
2014
HAPPY YEAR OF THE HORSE
Klein Dytham architecture
2015
HAPPY YEAR OF THE SHEEP
Klein Dytham architecture
DRAGON
KLEIN DYTHAM ARCHITECTURE
2012
THE YEAR OF THE DRAGON
STOP STRESSING OUT
SNAKE OIL
IDEA TONIC
PARTICULARLY PREPARED FOR CREATIVE PEOPLE BY KLEIN DYTHAM ARCHITECTURE
A BATHING KDA
2016
HAPPY YEAR OF THE MONKEY
Klein Dytham architecture
Wishing you a hot and spicy 2017 in the year of the
Rooster
TUONG OT SRIRACHA
Klein Dytham architecture
"spicing it up"
BONE-APPÉTIT
2018
YEAR OF THE
DOG

"Tokyo's first shared creative space"

DELUXE

Tokyo, Japan // Shared office space // 1998-2005

Deluxe, an underground cultural hub established in 1998, was the collective vision of six creative businesses that were outgrowing their tiny offices in Tokyo. Inspired by warehouse conversions in London and New York, KDa joined forces with design duo Namaiki, sound engineers Do Re Mi, interior designers Spinoff, DJ QuietStorm, and Tokyo Ale brewery to transform a former taxi garage in Azabu Juban into Tokyo's first flexible shared work and event space.

Offices were hidden behind a wall covered with the striking Deluxe logo, leaving an expansive open area for meetings, presentations, and collaborative events. Simple modular furnishings such as L-shaped partitions on casters, mobile benches, and tables allowed the space to be adaptable to any occasion.

Though it began as a venue for client transactions and business happenings, Deluxe swiftly evolved into a thought-provoking platform for multi-disciplinary artistic expression and boundary-pushing creativity. Events, scheduled to promote Tokyo Ale sales, invited a host of independent artists for improvised performances, experimental, music, and avant-garde exhibitions.

Boundaries were blurred—at one point, a weeklong art installation involved a woman sprinkling feathers over business meetings as she bathed naked in a tub of plumes suspended from the ceiling. Clients mingled with designers, artists, and musicians. Guests ran the gamut from the Dahm Triplets and Miss Universe Japan to groundbreaking musicians such as Keiji Haino, Morgan Fisher, and Lars Fredriksson's bizarre insect orchestra of a thousand crickets.

Within 5 years, events escalated in prestige and scale, as did the creative businesses behind Deluxe. When a fashion show thronged with over 400 guests, practical considerations necessitated a new chapter in Deluxe's evolution—the birth of SuperDeluxe, a venue dedicated to cultural events.

"The birthplace of PechaKucha Night"

SUPERDELUXE

Tokyo, Japan // Creative kitchen and noisy hole // 2002-2019

Like the original Deluxe taxi garage in Azabu Juban, SuperDeluxe's new Roppongi home was not a ready-made space for rent. The basement floor of a building earmarked for future redevelopment, it required substantial renovation to equip it with a fully functional bar and kitchen and, like its predecessor, modular furniture to ensure it could adapt to any event.

A live performance venue, bar, gallery, and lounge, SuperDeluxe remained true to its origins and introduced an eclectic roster of artists. Its location next to Roppongi Hills, a new residential and shopping complex within a rapidly evolving cultural landscape, was ideal. With Mike Kubeck and Tokyo Ale at its helm it became, literally and metaphorically, Tokyo's underground center of alternative exhibitions, concerts, fashion shows, and screenings—a melting pot of avant-garde artists, luminaries of experimental music, and high-profile celebrities.

Performers from the Fuji Rock Festival often dropped by for an extra gig as they passed through the capital, Fashion Week after-parties were held there, film stars visited, and pioneering artists that no other venue would take on finally found their audience.

It was also the birthplace of PechaKucha Night, KDa's speed-storytelling presentation platform for creatives, which became so successful it spawned international editions in more than 1,300 cities in over 140 countries.

By the time its building was finally scheduled for demolition, SuperDeluxe had hosted well over 5,000 events. Having to shutter its doors after 17 years in Roppongi only inspired the team to develop the concept further. In the face of shifting social priorities toward well-being, work-life balance and sustainable lifestyles during the COVID-19 pandemic, SuperDeluxe left the metropolis for the natural environs and local-community vibe of Kamogawa in Chiba Prefecture.

SABIAN

"A community hub of education, research, and shared experiences"

SUPERNATURALDELUXE

Chiba, Japan // Creative music minka and permaculture garden // 2022-

A two-hour train journey from Tokyo, in the heart of the coastal city of Kamogawa, SupernaturalDeluxe is a fresh new beginning for SuperDeluxe. Now housed in a registered cultural property of traditional wooden Japanese architecture and surrounded by lush greenery, it's a far cry from its city origins.

A collaboration between SuperDeluxe Director Mike Kubeck and Director of Permaculture AWA Phil Cashman, the ongoing restoration project aims to revitalize a *minka*, a traditional Japanese dwelling, and its vast grounds into a community hub of education, research, and shared experiences, as well as artistic, musical, and other creative expressions.

A former sake brewery is now the event space where local, national, and international guests are invited to perform against the rustic backdrop of wooden beams. A thatched roof house, its tatami-mat rooms, and original interiors offer a peaceful environment for artist residencies. Under the guidance of Cashman, a fertile garden is being cultivated into an allotment of sustainable crops.

With an emphasis on permaculture ethics, SupernaturalDeluxe plans include workshops and presentations on sustainable living, ecological care and nurturing community. Still a haven for independent artists, it has the space to be even more inclusive, with environmental activities, local events, and more.

"A global celebration of creativity"

PECHAKUCHA

Global // Presentation format // 1,300 cities and counting // 2003-

PechaKucha, a digital presentation platform and community that inspires and fosters creative dialogue via events in more than a thousand cities around the world, is one of KDa's greatest non-architectural achievements.

The idea was simple yet revolutionary: to develop a presentation format that would be dynamic, concise, and inclusive. Before the existence of YouTube, Instagram, TikTok, Vine, and the other social media platforms, PechaKucha, named after the Japanese onomatopoeic word for "chit chat," aspired to become a visual, physical social network open to all creative minds. Yet it had a humble inspiration: KDa's weekly show-and-tell office meetings.

Every Monday, to this day, KDa staff are encouraged to share their week's creative activities, from architectural sketches, project progress images, and factory visit experiences to weekend hobby pursuits and holiday snaps. As advances in digital photography and accessible software in the late 1990s made it easier for anyone to contribute, the meetings became an engaging way for KDa colleagues and collaborators to communicate and socialize before the work week ahead.

When KDa launched SuperDeluxe in 2003 and found itself under pressure to book more events to increase sales, Astrid, Mark, and Hisayama, KDa's main man, realized that their Monday meeting format could attract visitors to the space. One presenter would likely invite five or more friends, ten presenters potentially bringing in fifty to one hundred people. Planned as a monthly event on quiet weekdays at SuperDeluxe, PechaKucha Night was essentially a business idea, but with a key focus: to nurture a local creative community.

ONG KONG
BOGOTA
CHICAGO
SHANGHAI
BERLIN
NAMA
ZAPORIZHZHYA
MEXICO CITY
AALEN
DAMASCUS
EN
EL PASO
BEIJING
KUCHING
PRAGUE
TANIA
CLEVELAND
AARHUS
BRISBANE
ORNSKOLDSVIK
N JOSE, COSTA RICA
KABUL
BANGALORE
STOCKHOLM
BUENOS AIRES
CONCEPCIÓN
ZAGREB
DNIPROPETROVSK
MONTEVIDEO
THENBURG
ORLANDO
AUCKLAND
DUNDEE
GUANGZHOU
RCELONA
JERUSALEM
MURCIA
KYOTO
CANCUN
CAPETOWN
SCOW
PROVIDENCE
HYDERABAD
MIAMI
DICINE HAT
BEXHILL ON SEA
BILBAO
KAMPALA
SAN SEBASTIAN
CHRISTCHURCH
NIKKO
RUT
KHABAROVSK
OSLO
JOSEPH/BENTON HARBOR
LEIDEN
TEHRAN
PORTO
TEL AVIV

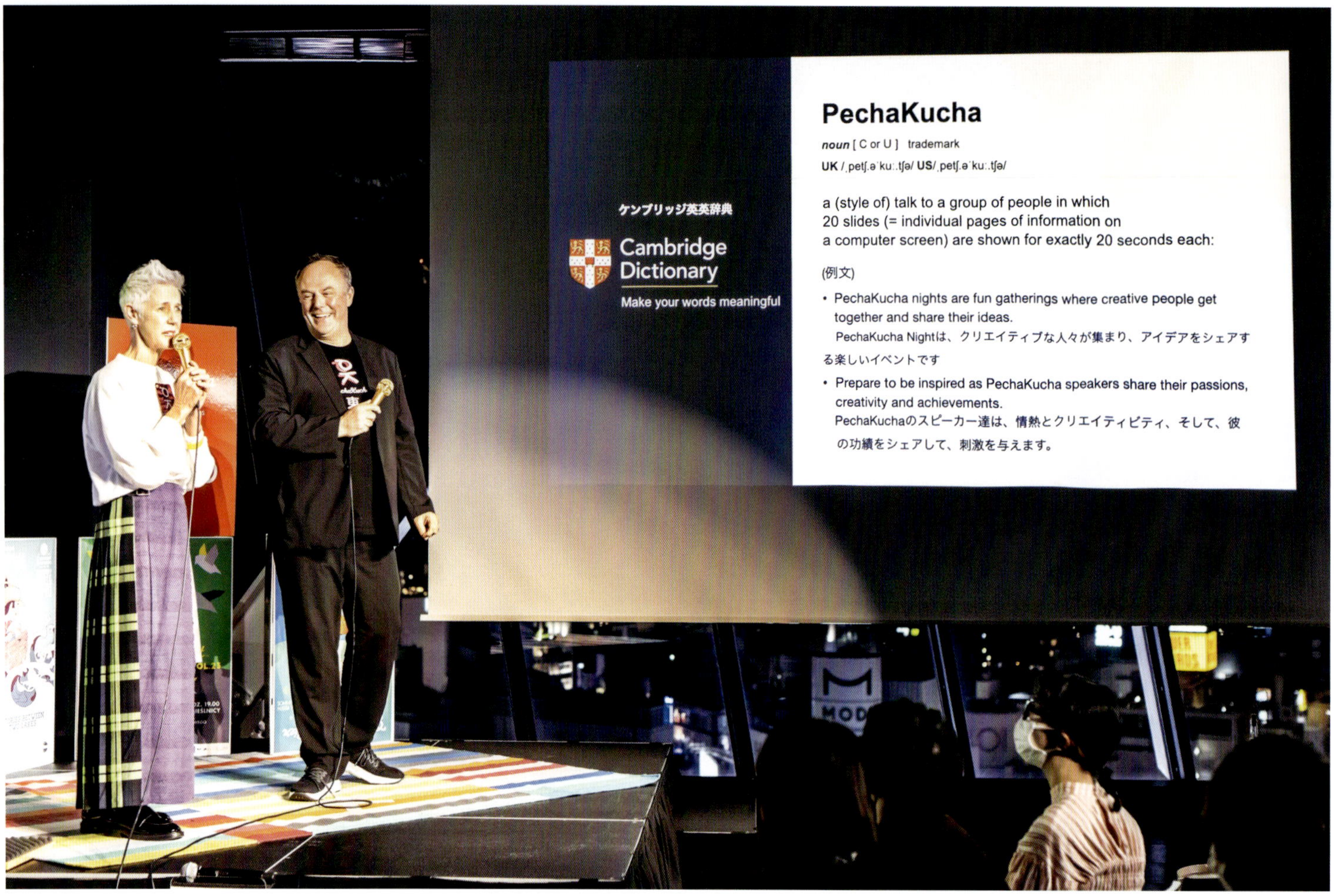

The famously short PechaKucha format—20 slides, 20 seconds per slide, a total of 6 minutes and 40 seconds per person—was initially devised to allow at least ten presenters fair floor time in one evening. Its ingenuity, however, lay in the constraints. To ensure every slide counted, presenters had to creatively select images and distill messages into bite-size portions, resulting in fast-paced and particularly engaging visual presentations. It was such an effective format that the word "pechakucha," defined as a "style of talk," was added to the Cambridge University Press dictionary, completely changing its original Japanese meaning.

The first SuperDeluxe PechaKucha held on February 20, 2003 was a modest gathering of KDa friends involving fourteen speakers. It was such a hit that visitors immediately began to enquire how they could also present. Within 3 years of running PechaKucha Nights in Tokyo, KDa was approached by enthusiasts hoping to establish events in other cities. In 2006, PechaKucha events were licensed in Los Angeles and Bern, swiftly followed by debuts in twenty other cities across the globe.

No matter the location or population, any city could apply for a license. As a nonprofit format, PechaKucha even brought positive moments of respite to poverty-stricken and war-torn countries. It developed hubs in metropolises but surprised all by thriving in tiny cities and unearthing the hidden creativity of little-known locations like Accident in the USA and Medicine Hat in Canada. Over 1,300 cities joined, each bringing together and celebrating local talent. In the Czech Republic, the events were so popular that two PechaKucha organizers were elected mayors of their cities.

Fundamental to PechaKucha's success is its inclusivity. It celebrates the creativity of any presenter—from renowned architects, artists, designers, and engineers to construction workers, amateur photographers, hobbyists, and unsung heroes of everyday life.

PechaKucha Nights became a fun way to discover a city's hidden local talent and personalities. Young architects or designers didn't need large bodies of work to present, entrepreneurs could share ideas, and individuals could express their personalities. In the early days, Mark's mother showcased her flower-arranging and cake-decorating skills, and Astrid's daughter, at age five, presented photos from her visit to London's Natural History Museum.

The speakers were eclectic and included private collectors, craft clubs, bakers, firefighters, and funeral directors. Some presentations were humorous or fascinatingly odd. An embroidery club revealed a selection of beautifully stitched soft porn. One guest presented his collection of Nana Mouskouri records—virtually identical but published in different countries. Others invited viewers behind the scenes of industries. A 63-year-old Japanese scaffolder left the audience gasping with admiration at his extraordinary photos taken from death-defying heights during the construction of Tokyo's Toranomon Hill complex.

PechaKucha

TOKYO DESIGNERS WEEK 2013
CREATiVE

INSPIRE
JAPAN
PechaKucha Night Cluj Editia 4
Inspire Japan
16 Aprilie 2011, ora 18:00
Ceainăria Sakura, Strada Moților 48
pechakucha-cluj.com
Facebook: PechaKucha Cluj
Intrare: 10 lei
24-FUN
VOL#5 APRIL 16 - 7PM - THE MADRAS CENTER
PechaKucha Night
chennai
facebook.com.pechakuchachennai
www.pknchennai.com
PechaKucha Night
TELE2
WWW.IDEALS.PH
PRESENT
PechaKucha Night
INSPIRE JAPAN
A GLOBAL PECHA KUCHA NIGHT EVENT WITH OVER 100 PARTICIPATING CITIES.
From Manila with Love
APRIL 16, 2011, 8PM
NOMNOMNOM
HAPPY FOOD
ADMISSION IS FREE
SPEAKERS
BIBOY HERNANDEZ
CHARLENE TAN
ELBERT OR
HERB FONDEVILLA
REIA AYUNAN
SARAH QUEBLATIN
TWEET SERING
PechaKucha Night
Maribor Vol.3
KDAJ SOBOTA
16. APRIL OB 20.20 URI
KJE MULTIMEDIJSKI
CENTER KIBLA
GLOBAL PECHAKUCHA DAY • VANCOUVER
PechaKucha Night Vancouver
SATURDAY APRIL 16
DOORS 4:00 • PRESENTATION 4:30
THE CASCADE ROOM • 2616 MAIN STREET
FREE ADMISSION • SUGGESTED DONATION $10*
http://www.pechakuchanightvancouver.com
ALL PROCEEDS BENEFIT ARCHITECTURE FOR HUMANITY'S REBUILD JAPAN PLANS • global-day.pecha-kucha.org
CLARK'S
PechaKucha Night
QUITO
VOLUMEN 3
PechaKucha
INSPIRE
JAPAN
architecture for humanity
Quito se suma apoyando a Japón en una noche muy interesante donde surtidos presentadores se expresan en distintos temas.
Sábado 16 de abril. 20h00.
Centro Cultural El Aguijón.
Tyler Spencer, didgeridoo en vivo.
www.pknquito.com
11
PechaKucha
INSPIR
JAPAN
architecture for human
TORSDAG 26. MAI KL. 19.3
STED: OLHALLEN
Helder Neves // architect // IceMusic Festival & Steinsvik arkitektkontor
Ragnhild Nessa // landscape architect // Urban Natur & Asplan Viak
Eva Bakkeslett // artist & cultivator
Berit Steenstrup // architect // 70°N arkitektur
Bjørn Eirik Olsen // Director & Aikido Sensei // Nofima & Tea, fish and
Peter W Søderman // architect // BC arkitektur
Michele Widerøe // interior designer // 70°N arkitektur
Alexander Muchenberger // artist // Bureau Detours
Torstein Piltingsrud // architect // Acona Technopole
70°N
tank
Mack
PechaKucha Night
Inspire
Japan
Inspire Japan
Roma Pechakucha Event
// 08.05.2011
// Roma_Forte Fanfulla
PECHA KUCHA NIGHT KOŠICE
TABAČKA KULTURFABRIK
16 4 2011 | 20.20 H
INSPIRE
JAPAN
GLOBAL PECHAKUCHA DAY / TORONT
BILBAO
PechaKucha
Night
16.04.2011
Aula de cultura BBK
20.20 h
sobota
16. 04. 2011
20:20 hod
design factory Bottova 2
Bratislava
PechaKucha
INSPIRE
JAPAN
architecture for humanity
PECHAKUCHA NIGHT
CORK #4
APRIL 20TH
CRANE LANE
20:00
TO SUPPORT ARCHITECTURE FOR HUMANITY AS PART OF PK INSPIRE JAPAN
Free entry : Fundraising for Japan
Are you interested in presenting?
INSPIRE
JAPAN
PechaKucha Night
KATHMANDU VOL#2
AS A PART OF GLOBAL PECHAKUCHA DAY
APRIL 16, 2011-SATURDAY 6:00PM ONWARDS
@ ATTIC BAR LAZIMPAT
PARTICIPATE+INSPIRE
DONATE+HELP JAPAN REBUILD
DOOR: 200/- 100/-
ALL PROCEEDS BENEFIT ARCHITECTURE FOR HUMANITY REBUILD JAPAN

In 2010, the catastrophic Haiti earthquake prompted the PechaKucha worldwide community to convene and explore its potential to aid humanity on a large scale. A 24-hour global brainstorming Skype session led to the PechaKucha Inspire Haiti project, which raised US$100,000 to build a school in the disaster area.

Just 1 month after the building's completion, the Tohoku earthquake and tsunami of 2011 devastated northeast Japan, and Inspire Japan was launched. Another US$100,000 was raised to build a sports center and shelters, and the PechaKucha Inspire initiative continued to document Tohoku's road to recovery. An ongoing global project, Inspire went on to fundraise for earthquake relief in Christchurch in 2011 and Nepal in 2015.

When COVID-19 posed a global threat, PechaKucha Inspire the World events—presentations of pandemic experiences, information, and creative solutions—were held, first in London and Manchester, then in twenty cities worldwide. PechaKucha Create, a new browser tool that allows anyone to create and publish a presentation online, kept the momentum during lockdowns, opening up the format to an even wider audience.

At time of writing, there are over 1,325 PechaKucha licensed cities worldwide, with key members bringing the global network together through regular online conferences and informal get-togethers.

The PechaKucha format is now an established tool in thousands of academic and educational institutions and businesses.

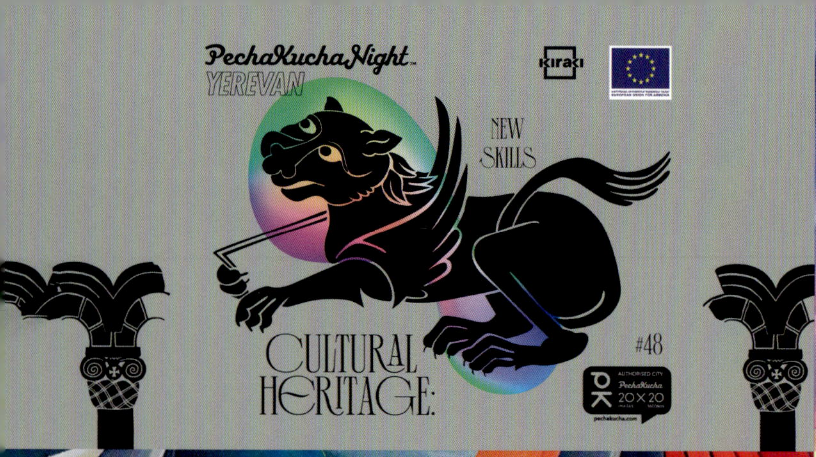
PechaKuchaNight
YEREVAN
NEW SKILLS
CULTURAL HERITAGE:
#48
pechakucha.com

PECHAKUCHA
42 SAN ANTONIO
KIMIYA FACTORY
ACTIVIST
ASHLEY BIRD
EDUCATOR/ENTREPRENEUR
JAMIE GONZALEZ
FOOD ACTIVIST
RANDALL RUDD
FILMMAKER/PROFESSOR
OSCAR ALVARADO
MOSAICIST/SCULPTOR
COLLEEN SWAIN
DIRECTOR
THEATRE

PechaKuchaNight
PKN Naha
#2
@okimu
POWERED BY
PechaKucha
20×20
IMAGES SECONDS
pechakucha.com
2023
5.27
sat

PechaKuchaNight SHANGHAI
2024.11.07

PechaKuchaNight
上海
2025.02.13
19H
22H
SPEAKERS
BILL GLENNIE
VAIBHAV GUPTA
THOMAS DERKSEN
WENWEN
KUAN TONG
NOODLES
JUAN
DAN ZHU

SHIFTING
GEARS
Wednesday May 31st
THE OASIS AT LOST VALLEY PIZZ
DOORS AT 7:20 PM
PechaKuchaNight
PROVIDENCE

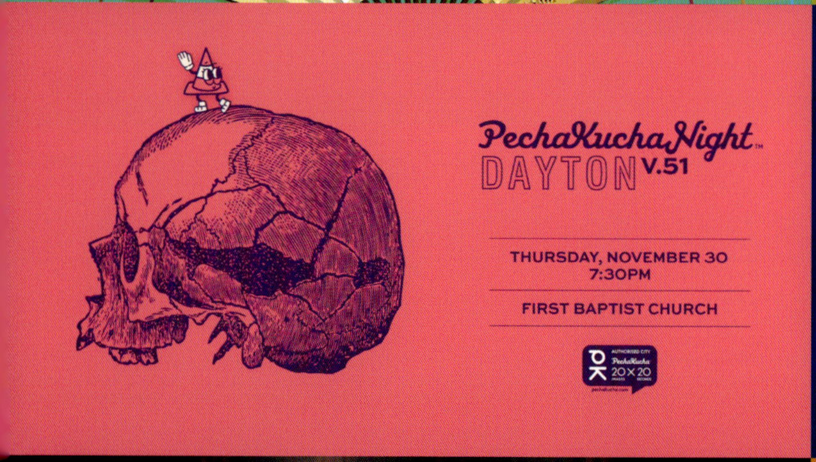
PechaKuchaNight
DAYTON V.51
THURSDAY, NOVEMBER 30
7:30PM
FIRST BAPTIST CHURCH

قريباً
20X20
NOW PechaKuchaNight Aden 20X20
STAY TUNED
POWERED BY GOLOBAL SHAPERS
COMMUNITY ADEN

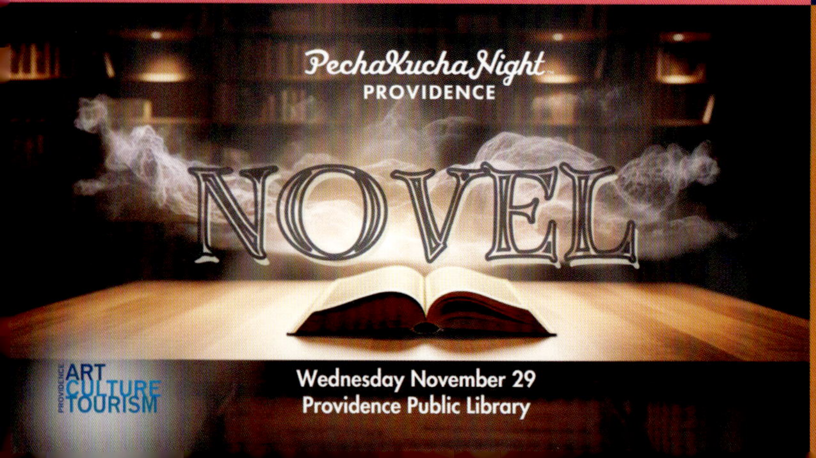
PechaKuchaNight
PROVIDENCE
NOVEL
ART CULTURE TOURISM
Wednesday November 29
Providence Public Library

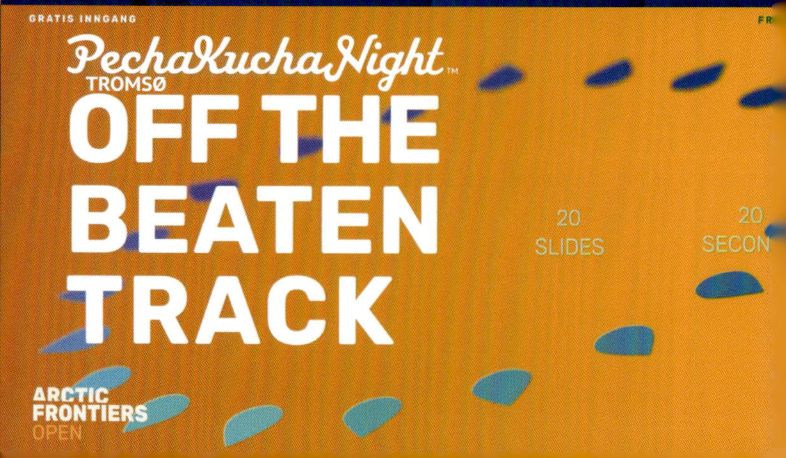
GRATIS INNGANG
PechaKuchaNight
TROMSØ
OFF THE
BEATEN
TRACK
20
SLIDES
ARCTIC
FRONTIERS
OPEN

chaKucha Night
KARTA VOL.47
ORGANIZED BY
Maverick
MIND OVER MATTER
4 MAY 2023
FREE & OPEN FOR PUBLIC
AUTHORISED CITY
PechaKucha
20×20
LIVE on youtube.com/
maverickindonesia

PechaKucha
Johannesburg
Vol. 31

PechaKucha
DESIGNART
TOKYO
TOKYO
aking SPARKS Fly
chaKucha x DESIGNART Tokyo
th OCTOBER @ The CORE KITCHEN / SPACE
0pm Open 7.30pm Presentations

JOLT PRESENTS:
PechaKucha Night
GLOUCESTER
A NIGHT OF QUICKFIRE TALKS ON CREATIVE TOPICS BY CREATIVE PEOPLE
MAY 10TH 2023|
6PM - 8 PM
WAREHOUSE 4
JOLTGLOUCESTER.COM
GLOUCESTERBREWERY.CO.UK
JOLT
POWERED BY
PechaKucha
20×20

2 0 2 4 . 0 9 . 2 0
PechaKucha Night x
敢于颠覆 DARE TO DISRUPT

PechaKucha Night
LONDON
Play
VOL. 36
AUTHORIZED CITY
PechaKucha
20×20

PechaKucha Night
PROVIDENCE
OUT OF THE BAG
Haus of Codec
Wednesday
June 26
The Industrious
Spirit Company

PechaKucha Night
Dundee Vol. 30

AUTHORISED CITY
PechaKucha
20×20
PechaKucha Night
LIBEREC vol. 12
28/11/23
VARŠAVA
#ARCHITEKTURA #FILM #DÁRCOVSTVÍ
POKRAČOVÁNÍ
PŘÍŠTĚ...

PechaKucha Night
ASHEVILLE
33
FEB 16
DOORS 7P
THE GROVE HOUSE
11 GROVE STREET
pechakuchaavl.org/attend
POWERED BY
PechaKucha
20×20

1,237 PECHAKUCHA CITIES AS OF SPRING 2025 A CORUÑA AALBORG AALEN AARHUS ABBOTSFORD ABERDE
AJDOVSCINA AKRON AKTAU AKTOBE AL-KHOBAR ALBANY, CA ALBANY, GA ALBANY, NY ALBUQUERQ
ALMERÍA ÄLMHULT AMBATO AMERSFOORT AMHERST AMMAN AMSTERDAM ANCHORAGE ANDORRA ÄNGELHOL
ASAHIKAWA ASHEVILLE ASHLAND ASTANA (NUR-SULTAN) ASTEN ASTRAKHAN ASUNCION ATHENS ATHENS, C
AZORES BACOLOD BAD KREUZNACH BADAJOZ BAHIA BLANCA BAKU BALATON-FELVIDÉK BALI BALLAR
BARCELONA BARDEJOV BARI BARILOCHE BARNAUL BARNSLEY BARQUISIMETO BARRANQUILLA BARRY BAS
BEIHAI BEIJING BEIRUT BELFAST BELGOROD BELGRADE BELLINGHAM, WA BELO HORIZONTE BEMIDJI BENEŠ
BIEL BIELEFELD BIENNE BILBAO BILLINGS, MT BILOXI BIRMINGHAM BIRSTEIN BISHKEK BLANTYRE BLUE HIL
BOONE BORÅS BORDEAUX BOSTON BOULDER BOURNEMOUTH BOWDOINHAM BOWLING GREEN BOZEMA
BRESCIA BREZNO BRIDGEND BRIDGEPORT BRIDGETOWN BRIDLINGTON BRIGHTON BRISBANE BRISTOL BRN
BUDAÖRS BUDAPEST BUDE BUENOS AIRES BUFFALO BUJUMBURA BULAWAYO BURGAS BURLINGTON,
CALTANISSETTA CAMBRIDGE CANBERRA CANCÚN CANMORE CANNON FALLS CANTON CAPE TOWN CARAC
CEDAR RAPIDS CESKE BUDEJOVICE CHAMPAIGN-URBANA CHANDIGARH CHARLESTON CHARLOTTE CHATTANOO
CHEWELAH CHIANG MAI CHIAYI CHIBA CHICAGO CHICHESTER CHICLAYO CHICO CHICOUTIMI CHIHUAHU
COLIMA COLLEGE STATION COLLINGWOOD COLOGNE COLOMBO COLONIA COLUMBIA, MO COLUMBIA,
CÓRDOBA CORK COROWA COTONOU COVENTRY CRANBROOK CRATO CREVILLENT CÚCUTA CUIABÁ CURITI
SALAAM DARKHAN DARTMOOR DARWIN DAVAO DAVENPORT DAWSON CITY DAYBORO DAYTON, MN DAYTO
DOHA DONCASTER DONETSK DONGGUAN DOORN DORNBIRN DORTMUND DOUGLAS DRESDEN DUBAI DUBL
DURANGO, CO DURBAN DURHAM DUSHANBE DÜSSELDORF EAST LONDON EASTON EASTSOUND EDINBURG
ENSENADA ERBIL ERFURT ERLANGEN ESBJERG ESKIŞEHIR ESSLINGEN EUGENE EUREKA, MT EVANSTON EXET
FORSTER FORT COLLINS FORT LAUDERDALE FORT MCMURRAY FORT MYERS FORT SMITH FORT WORTH FOZ D
FUKUOKA FUKUSHIMA FULLERTON FUNCHAL FUNDÃO FUZHOU GAINESVILLE, FL GALASHIELS GALW
GISBORNE GLASGOW GLAZOV GLIWICE GLOUCESTER GOLD COAST GOLDENDALE GOODYEAR GORE GORG
GRENLAND GREYMOUTH GRONINGEN GUADALAJARA GUANAJUATO GUANGZHOU GUATEMALA CITY GUAYAQU
HAMAMATSU HAMBURG HAMEDAN HAMILTON, NEW ZEALAND HAMILTON, ON HAMPTONS HANGZHOU HAN
HELENA HELSINGBORG HELSINGØR HELSINKI HENGELO HERAKLION HERMOSILLO HILDESHEIM HILVERSU
HOUSTON HOUTEN HRADEC KRÁLOVÉ HUANCAYO HUDDERSFIELD HUELVA HUMPOLEC HUNTSVILLE HYDERABA
ISLAMABAD ISTANBUL IZHEVSK IZMIR JACKSON, MS JACKSON, NH JACKSON, TN JACKSONVILLE JAÉN JAFFR
JUÁREZ KABUL KADNIKOV KAGOSHIMA KAISERSLAUTERN KALAMAZOO KALININGRAD KALISPELL KAMLOO
KAUNAS KAWASAKI KAWERAU KAYSERI KAZAN KELOWNA KEMEROVO KENDAL KENNEBUNKPORT KERIKE
KIRISHIMA KIRUNA KITAKYUSHU KLADNO KLAIPEDA KLATOVY KNOXVILLE KOBE KOBLENZ KOCHI KOLDIN
KRISTIANSAND KRISTIANSTAD KUALA LUMPUR KUCHING KUMAMOTO KUNGSBACKA KUNMING KUOPIO KUR
LA RIOJA LAAYOUNE LAFAYETTE LAGOS LAGUNA BEACH LAHOLM LAHORE LAKE RIDGE LAKELAND LAMBERTVILL
LAS PALMAS LAS VEGAS LATINA LATTAKIA LAUNCESTON LAUSANNE LE BLANC LEAMINGTON SPA LECCE LEE
LERWICK LEUVEN LEWISTON LEXINGTON LIBEREC LIBREVILLE LIÈGE LIENZ LILLE LILONGWE LIMA LIMERI
LLANDUDNO LLOYDMINSTER LOCKHART LODZ LOGROÑO LONDON LONDON, ON LONG BEACH LONGMON
LUEBECK LULEÅ LUND LUSAKA LUXEMBOURG LVOV (LVIV) LYON MAASTRICHT MADISON, WI MADR
NH MANCHESTER, VT MANDALAY MANILA MANIZALES MANSFIELD, OH MAPUTO MAR DEL PLATA MARACA
PROVENCE MARTHA'S VINEYARD MARTIN MASERU MASHHAD MAURITIUS MAZATLÁN MEDAN MEDELL
MIAMI CLEVELAND MIDCOAST MIDDELBURG MIKKELI MILAN MILTON KEYNES MILWAUKEE MINNEAPOLIS MIN
MONTEMORELOS MONTERREY MONTEVIDEO MONTPELIER, VT MONTPELLIER MONTREAL MORIOKA MORRILTO
MURWILLUMBAH MUSCAT MUSCATINE MYRTLE BEACH NABEREZHNYE CHELNY NABLUS NAGANO NAGOYA NAH
NASHVILLE NEIVA NELSON, BC NELSON, NEW ZEALAND NELSON MANDELA BAY NEUQUÉN NEW BERN NE
NEWCASTLE UPON TYNE NEWLAND NEWTOWN NICE NICOSIA NIIGATA NIKKO NILES NILÜFER NISHINOMI
NORWICH, CT NORWICH, UK NOTTINGHAM NOVI SAD NOVOKUZNETSK NOVOSIBIRSK NOVÝ HROZENK
OLSZTYN OLYMPIA OMAHA OMSK OPOLE OPOTIKI ÖREBRO ORENBURG ORIHUELA ORLANDO ÖRNSKÖLDSV
OTTAWA OUAGADOUGOU OULU OURENSE OWENSBORO OXFORD PACE PADERBORN PADOVA PAISL
PARIS PARRAMATTA PASTO PATCHOGUE PAVLODAR PAWTUCKET PEEL PEKANBARU PENANG PENSACOL
PHILLIP ISLAND PHOENIX PINAMAR PINGTUNG PISA PÍSEK PITTSBORO PITTSBURG, KS PITTSBURGH, P
PORT OF SPAIN PORTALEGRE PORTIMÃO PORTLAND, ME PORTLAND, OR PORTO PORTO ALEGRE PORTSMOUT
PRISTINA PROVIDENCE PUEBLA PUEBLO, CO PUERTO MADRYN PUERTO VALLARTA PUNE PYATIGORSK KALMA
RAGUSA RALEIGH RAPID CITY RECIFE REDDING REDWOOD CITY REGENSBURG REGINA, SK RESISTENCIA REYKJAV
ROCKFORD ROME ROORKEE ROSARIO ROSENHEIM ROSTOV-ON-DON ROTHERHAM ROTTERDAM ROVIGO RUGE
SPRING ISLAND SALVADOR SALZBURG SAMARA SAN ANTONIO SAN CRISTÓBAL DE LA LAGUNA SAN DIEGO SA
OBISPO SAN PEDRO SULA SAN SALVADOR SAN SEBASTIÁN SANA'A SANDEFJORD SANT PERE DE RIBES SAN
SANTANDER SANTIAGO SANTO DOMINGO SANTOS SÃO JOSÉ DOS CAMPOS SÃO PAULO SAPPORO SARAJEV
SECHELT SEGORBE SEINÄJOKI SEMARANG SENDAI SENIGALLIA SEOUL SEVASTOPOL SEVERODVINSK SEVILL
SHIZUOKA CITY SHODOSHIMA SHONAN SHYMKENT SILVER SPRING SINGAPORE SIOUX FALLS SKAGASTRÖN
ANTIPOLIS SORIA SOSNOWIEC SOUTHEND-ON-SEA SPLIT SPRINGFIELD, IL SPRINGFIELD, MO SPRINGFIELD, C
NEOTS ST. PAUL ST. PETERSBURG STAFFORDSHIRE STARÁ ĽUBOVŇA STARACHOWICE STAUNTON STAVANG
STURGIS STUTTGART SULPHUR BLUFF ŠUMPERK SUNDSVALL SUNSHINE COAST SURABAYA SURAKARTA (SOL
TAGBILARAN TAGUIG TAICHUNG TAINAN TAIPEI TALLAHASSEE TALLINN TAMALE TAMPA BAY TAMPE
TEGUCIGALPA TEL AVIV TELFORD TEMPE TENERIFE TERUEL THE HAGUE THESSALONIKI THIRROUL THREE OAK
TØNDER TOPEKA TORONTO TORREÓN TÓRSHAVN TOULOUSE TOURNAI TOWNSVILLE TOYAMA TOYOOK
TRONDHEIM TROYES TRUCKEE TRUJILLO TSU TSURUOKA TULA TULSA TULUM TUNIS TURIN TURKISTA
LABEM UTRECHT UTSUNOMIYA UZICE VAASA VADUZ VALAŠSKÉ MEZIŘÍČÍ VALENCIA VALENCIA, VE VALLADOL
VERMILLION VESZPRÉM VICTORIA VIENNA VIENTIANE VIGO VILLARS-SUR-OLLON VILNIUS VIMPERK VIN
VOLOGDA VOLTA REDONDA VYKSA WACO WAGGA WAGGA WAKEFIELD WALTHAM FOREST WANAKA WANGAN
WESLEY CHAPEL WEST KILBRIDE WEST PALM BEACH WESTPORT, CT WHANGAREI WHISTLER WHITEHORSE WILKE
WISMAR WOERDEN WOLFVILLE WORCESTER WORTHING WROCLAW WUHAN WUPPERTAL XÁBIA XALAP
YOGYAKARTA YOKOHAMA YORK YORK, PA YOUNGSTOWN YSTAD YUEYANG ZAGREB ZAPORIZHZHY

BILENE ABU DHABI ABUJA ACCIDENT ACCRA ADELAIDE ADEN AGRIGENTO AGUASCALIENTES AHMEDABAD
LBURY-WODONGA ALEPPO ALEXANDRA ALEXANDRIA ALGIERS ALICANTE ALICE SPRINGS ALKMAAR ALMATY
NKARA ANTALYA APPLETON ARCATA ÅRE ARENDAL AREQUIPA ARIANA ARIMA ARNHEM ARTHOG ÅS
THERTON ATLANTA ATLANTIC CITY ATYRAU AUCKLAND AUGSBURG AURORA AUSTIN AVEIRO AVILA AVILÉS
ALTIMORE BANDAR SERI BEGAWAN BANDUNG BANGALORE BANGKOK BANGOR, ME BANGOR, UK BANJA LUKA
ASINGSTOKE BASKING RIDGE BATAVIA BATON ROUGE BÁTOVCE BEACON BEAUFORT, SC BEDFORD BEECHWORTH
ERGEN BERKELEY BERLIN BERMUDA BERN BERWICK-UPON-TWEED BEXHILL-ON-SEA BIALYSTOK BIDDEFORD
IE BLUE MOUNTAINS BOBO-DIOULASSO BODØ BODRUM BOGOTA BOLINGBROOK BOLOGNA BOLZANO BONN
RAGA BRADFORD BRAGANÇA BRAMPTON BRASÍLIA BRATISLAVA BRATTLEBORO, VT BRAUNSCHWEIG BREDA
ROOKINGS BROOKLYN BROOME BRUNSWICK BRUNTÁL BRUSSELS BRYAN BUCARAMANGA BUCHAREST
URNABY BURSA BUTTE BYDGOSZCZ BYTČA CÁDIZ CAGAYAN DE ORO CAGLIARI CAIRNS CAIRO CALGARY CALI
ARAGUATATUBA CARDIFF CASABLANCA CASTELLÓN DE LA PLANA CASTLEMAINE CATANIA CAXIAS DO SUL CEBU
HEBOKSARY CHELMSFORD CHELTENHAM CHELYABINSK CHENGDU CHENNAI CHEONGJU CHEREPOVETS
HILLICOTHE CHISINAU CHITA CHOLULA CHRISTCHURCH CINCINNATI CIREBON CLUJ-NAPOCA COIMBRA
OLUMBUS COLWYN BAY COMO COMOX VALLEY CONCEPCIÓN COOKTOWN COPENHAGEN COQUITLAM
YPRUS CZĘSTOCHOWA DAEGU DALI DALLAS DALS LÅNGED DAMASCUS DANANG DANVILLE, KY DAR ES
H DEL MAR DENIZLI DENVER DERBY DES MOINES DESSAU DETROIT DEWSBURY DHAKA DINKELSBÜHL DNIPRO
UBNA DUBUQUE DULUTH DUMAGUETE DUNDEE DUNEDIN DUNFERMLINE DUNSBOROUGH DURANGO, MEXICO
DMONTON EGG HARBOR EINDHOVEN EKATERINBURG EL PASO ELGIN ELIZABETHTOWN ELLENSBURG ENSCHEDE
AIRBANKS FAIRFIELD FALKENBERG FARGO FARO FAYETTEVILLE FERROL FITCHBURG FLAGSTAFF FLINT FLORENCE
UAÇU FRANKFURT FREDERICK FREDERIKSHAVN FRESNO FRIBOURG FROSINONE FUERTEVENTURA-LANZAROTE
ARRISON GÄVLE GDANSK GEELONG GENÈVE GENOVA GHENT GIBSONS GIJON GINOWAN GIRARDOT GIRONA
OTHENBURG GÖTTINGEN GRANADA GRAND RAPIDS GREENOCK GREENSBORO GREENVILLE GREENWICH
UILDFORD GUIMARÃES GURGAON GWALIOR GWANGJU HACHINOHE HAIFA HAKATA HALIFAX HALMSTAD
ANOVER HARARE HARPERS FERRY HARRISBURG HARTFORD HARTSVILLE HASTINGS HAVANA HEFER VALLEY
IROSHIMA HJØRRING HO CHI MINH CITY HOBART HÖGANÄS HOI AN HONG KONG HONOLULU HOPEWELL
SI IBAGUE ILIGAN ILOILO INDIANAPOLIS INDORE INNSBRUCK INVERNESS IOANNINA IPOH IRKUTSK
AIPUR JAKARTA JEDDAH JERSEY JERSEY CITY JERUSALEM JIHLAVA JOHANNESBURG JOINVILLE JÖNKÖPING
AMPALA KANDY KANSAS CITY KARACHI KARAGANDY KARLSRUHE KATHMANDU KATOWICE KATRINEHOLM
HABAROVSK KHARKOV KHARTOUM KHMELNYTSKYI KHOURIBGA KIGALI KILKENNY KINGSTON KINSHASA
OLKATA KONGSBERG KONSTANZ KOSICE KOSTANAY KOSZALIN KOTA KINABALU KRAKÓW KRASNOYARSK
URUME KUTA UTARA KUWAIT CITY KYIV KYOTO KYZYLORDA LA CONNER LA PAZ, BOLIVIA LA PAZ, MÉXICO
EW HOPE LANCASTER LANDSKRONA LANGNAU LANKARAN LANSING LANZAROTE ARRECIFE LARGO LARNACA
EESBURG LEEUWARDEN LEFKOŞA LEICESTER LEIDEN LEKSAND LEÓN, SPAIN LEÓN, MEXICO LEONARDTOWN
MOGES LINCOLN, NE LINCOLN, UK LINKÖPING LINZ LISBON LISBURN LIUZHOU LIVERPOOL LJUBLJANA
ONGUEUIL LOS ANGELES LOS SANTOS DE MAIMONA LOUISVILLE LOULÉ LOW... LUCERNE

... and BEYOND

AKASSAR MALAGA MALANG MALDEN MALLORCA MALMÖ MANADO MANAMA MANCHESTER MANCHESTER,
ARAMAG MARIÁNSKÉ LÁZNĚ MARIBOR MARIEHAMN MARKHAM MARQUETTE MARSASCALA MARSEILLE-
EDICINE HAT MELBOURNE MEMPHIS, TN MENDOZA MERANO MERIDA MÉRIDA MERSIN METEPEC MEXICO CITY
INSK MISSISSAUGA MISSOULA MLADÁ BOLESLAV MONCTON MONHEGAN MONROVIA MONS MONTCLAIR
OSCOW MOSCOW, ID MOUNT FOREST MUENSTER MUKALLA MUMBAI MUNICH MURCIA MURMANSK
AIROBI NAKHCHIVAN NAKURU NANAIMO NANCY NANNING NANTES NAPIER NAPLES NARA NARAMATA
ELHI NEW HAVEN NEW ORLEANS NEW PLYMOUTH NEW WESTMINSTER NEW YORK NEWCASTLE, AUSTRALIA
ITRA NIVALA NIZHNY NOVGOROD NOIDA NOORDWIJK NORFOLK NORMAN NORRKÖPING NORTH BERWICK
UREMBERG NYMBURK OAKLAND OAXACA ODENSE ODESSA OITA OKAYAMA OKLAHOMA CITY OLOMOUC
SAKA OSIJEK OSLO OSNABRUECK OSOYOOS OSSETT OSTEND ÖSTERSUND ØSTFOLD OSTRAVA OTSU
ALERMO PALMA DE MALLORCA PALMERSTON NORTH PALO ALTO PAMPLONA-IRUÑA PANAMÁ PANJIM PARANÁ
ENTICTON PEORIA PERM PERTH PERUGIA PERVOURALSK PESCARA PETALING JAYA PETERBOROUGH PHILADELPHIA
TTSFIELD PLOVDIV PLZEŇ PODGORICA POITIERS PONTEVEDRA POPRAD PORDENONE PORI PORT COQUITLAM
H PORTSMOUTH, UK POZNAN PRAGUE PRESCOTT PRESOV PRETORIA PRINCE EDWARD COUNTY PRINCE GEORGE
INGDAO QUEBEC QUEENSTOWN QUERETARO QUETZALTENANGO QUILPUÉ QUITO RABAT RADCLIFFE RAGLAN
CHMOND, BC RICHMOND, VA RIGA RIJEKA RIMINI RIO DE JANEIRO RISØR RIVERSIDE RIVNE RIYADH ROANOKE
YE SACRAMENTO SAIKI SAINT JOHN SAINT-ETIENNE ŠAĽA SALAMANCA SALISBURY SALT LAKE CITY SALT
ERNANDO SAN FRANCISCO SAN JOSÉ SAN JOSE, CA SAN JUAN, ARGENTINA SAN JUAN, PUERTO RICO SAN LUIS
ARBARA SANTA CRUZ DE LA SIERRA SANTA CRUZ, CA SANTA FE, ARGENTINA SANTA FE, NM SANTA TECLA
ARATOGA SPRINGS SASKATOON SATSUMA-SENDAI SAULT STE. MARIE SAVANNAH SCHIEDAM SCRANTON SEATTLE
FAX SHANGHAI SHARJAH SHEFFIELD SHENYANG SHENZHEN SHERBROOKE SHERWOOD PARK SHIMODATE
KOPJE SKÖVDE SNOWMASS VILLAGE SOCHI SOFIA SOKOL SOKOLOV SOLOTHURN SOMERVILLE SOPHIA
T. ALBERT ST. ANDREWS ST. AUGUSTINE ST. CLOUD ST. GALLEN ST. JOHN'S ST. JOSEPH ST. LOUIS ST. LUCIA ST.
TELLENBOSCH STILLWATER STIRLING STOCKHOLM STOKE-ON-TRENT STONINGTON STORD STRAKONICE
URAT SURGUT SURREY SUŠICE SVENDBORG SWINDON SYDNEY SYDNEY, NS SYSERT SZCZECIN TACOMA
ANGERANG TANJUNG PINANG TAOS TARAZ TARRAGONA TASHKENT TAURANGA TBILISI TECKOMATORP
ANJIN TIJUANA TILBURG TINGVOLL TIRANA TOKUSHIMA TOKYO TOLEDO, OH TOLYATTI TOMAR TOMSK
RAVERSE CITY TRELEW TRENČÍN TRENTO TREVISO TRIESTE TŘINEC TRIPOLI TRNAVA TROLLHÄTTAN TROMSØ
URKU TYUMEN UBUD UDINE UFA UHERSKE HRADISTE ULAANBAATAR ULLADULLA UMEÅ UPPSALA ÚSTÍ NAD
ALLETTA VALPARAÍSO VANCOUVER VARASE VARBERG VÄSTERÅS VÄXJÖ VEENENDAAL VEJLE VENICE
EL MAR VISBY VITÓRIA VITORIA-GASTEIZ VLADIKAVKAZ VLADIMIR VLADIVOSTOK VODŇANY VOLGOGRAD
ARSAW WARWICK WASHINGTON D.C. WATERLOO WATERVILLE, ME WATERVILLE, NY WEIMAR WELLINGTON
ARRE WILLIAMSBURG WINCHESTER WINDHOEK WINDSOR WINNIPEG WINSTON-SALEM WINTER HARBOR
AN XIAMEN YAKIMA YAKUTSK YAMAGUCHI YANGON YAROSLAVL YAZD YELLOWKNIFE YEREVAN YEYSK
ARAGOZA ZDAR NAD SAZAVOU ZEITZ ŽELEZNÝ BROD ZHUHAI ZILINA ZLÍN ZNOJMO ZOETERMEER ZÜRICH

コブラ会
COBRA KDA
ONE TEAM, ONE SPIRIT, ONE GOAL
1 JANUARY 2025
KDAFLIX
GLOBAL RELEASE

About KDa

Klein Dytham architecture (KDa) is a multidisciplinary design practice known for its dynamic approach to architecture, interiors, public spaces, installations, and global events. Established in Tokyo in the early 1990s by Royal College of Art graduates Astrid Klein and Mark Dytham, and joined by Yukinari Hisayama in 1996, KDa has built a reputation for creating innovative and engaging environments that seamlessly blend functionality with bold, colorful and vibrant aesthetics.

Among KDa's most acclaimed projects are Daikanyama T-SITE and Open House in Bangkok, both recognized by the *Financial Times* as among twenty of the most beautiful bookstores in the world. Its portfolio continues to expand, with recent notable works including Fender's Flagship Tokyo, an inventive hinoki wood façade for Cartier in Osaka, and a state-of-the-art music gallery for KEF Music Gallery in Tokyo.

KDa's work has garnered numerous prestigious awards, including the Dezeen Award for Best Hotel and Short-stay Interior Hotel (2021) and Best Hospitality Space (2021). The studio won the World Architecture Festival Award for Best Shopping Centre (2012), Cultural Building of the Year (2015), Small Project of the Year (2023), and Retail Project of the Year (2024), and has won the Design for Asia Grand Prize three times, an unprecedented achievement.

In 2003, KDa launched PechaKucha Night, a Tokyo-based event for designers to showcase their work, which has since evolved into a global phenomenon with events in more than 1,300 cities, inspiring creatives worldwide.

KDa also co-founded DESIGNART, Tokyo's premier design and art festival, and is deeply committed to community-focused initiatives. Astrid and Mark are active board members of HOME-FOR-ALL, a nonprofit organization dedicated to building community spaces in areas of Japan affected by natural disasters. Currently, KDa is actively involved in the Noto region, which was struck by a significant earthquake in January 2024.

KDa's unwavering dedication to design excellence and community-building continues to make a profound impact on the global creative landscape.

Klein Dytham architecture // www.klein-dytham.com

PechaKucha Night // www.pechakucha.com

Principals

Astrid Klein

Astrid Klein was born in Italy in 1962, educated in France and the UK, and since 1988 has lived and worked in Japan. After graduating from the Royal College of Art in London, Astrid was drawn to Japan by the simplicity of design, attention to detail, and the freedom from traditional constraints. In Tokyo she began working for Toyo Ito and in 1991 she co-founded Klein Dytham architecture with Mark Dytham.

Astrid is a sought-after speaker internationally. She has been a visiting lecturer at Berkeley University, and has taught at Nihon University and Musashino University in Tokyo. Currently, she is teaching at Toyo Ito's Architecture School for Kids. She is a board member of HOME-FOR-ALL, an initiative to build community hubs in earthquake- and tsunami-affected areas of Japan, and co-founder of DESIGNART, a design and art festival in Tokyo.

Mark Dytham MBE

Born in the UK in 1964, Mark studied architecture at the University of Newcastle and the Royal College of Art in London. In 1988, he travelled with his business partner, Astrid Klein, to Tokyo, and together they found work with Toyo Ito. They soon established Klein Dytham architecture, working freely across disciplines, including architecture, interiors, furniture, installations, and events.

He is a board member of HOME-FOR-ALL and co-founder of DESIGNART. Along with Astrid and Hisayama, they devised PechaKucha Night in 2003, which is now a ubiquitous presentation format for creatives globally.

Mark is a frequent guest speaker at international design events, has taught at universities in Japan and beyond, and in 2000 was awarded an MBE (Member of the British Empire) by Queen Elizabeth II for services to British design in Japan.

Yukinari Hisayama

Born in 1973 in Ako, Hyogo, Japan, Hisayama is a licensed architect and interior designer with a Bachelor of Architecture from Yokohama National University. He has been with Klein Dytham architecture since 1996. His deep understanding of the KDa approach complements his broad experience in all phases of the design process and extensive knowledge of materials and construction. He brings a strong artistic sensibility to his position as the most senior member of KDa. He has been directly or indirectly involved in nearly all of KDa's projects and was the person who named PechaKucha! He is currently teaching at Kanto Gakuen University and Kuwasawa Design School, and is also taking a strong lead raising the awareness of HOME-FOR-ALL through seminars and conferences in Japan.

Awards

2024

World Architecture Festival, INSIDE Retail Project of the Year, Fender Flagship Tokyo

2023

World Architecture Festival, Small Project of the Year, Karuizawa Commongrounds

Jiyugaoka Landscape Award, G-Building, Jiyugaoka

2022

Good Design Award, MONE Group Office, Tokyo

Architizer A+Awards, Architecture + Branding Category, Cartier Façade, Osaka

2021

Dezeen Awards 2021, Hotel and Short-stay Interior of the Year, Toggle Hotel, Tokyo

Dezeen Awards 2021, Hospitality Building of the Year, PokoPoko Clubhouse, Nasu

British Chamber of Commerce Japan, Company of the Year, Klein Dytham architecture

2019

ICSC Global Awards VIVA, Retail Category, Grand Prize, Open House, Bangkok

2018

Mapic Awards, Best Leisure Concept in a Retail Space, Open House, Bangkok

Good Design Award, Open House, Bangkok

Asian Bookstore Forum, The Most Well Designed Bookstore, Open House, Bangkok

World Architecture News, Façade Award, Ginza Place, Tokyo

World Architecture News, Waterfront Award, Picchio Visitors Centre, Karuizawa

2017

Design for Asia Award, Grand Award, Open House, Bangkok

2016

Design for Asia Award, Grand Award, Gallery TOTO, Narita Airport

2015

Ministry of Land, Infrastructure and Transport, Toilet of the Year, Gallery TOTO, Narita Airport

World Architecture Festival Award, World Cultural Building, Home-for-All, Soma City

2013

Wallpaper* Design Awards, Best Bookshop, Daikanyama T-SITE, Tokyo

2012

Design for Asia Award, Grand Award, Daikanyama T-SITE, Tokyo

World Architecture Festival, Best Shopping Centre Award, Daikanyama T-SITE, Tokyo

American Retail Environment Awards, Grand Prize, Sony Store, Los Angeles

2008

British Chamber of Commerce Japan, Corporate Innovation Award, Klein Dytham architecture

2007

Ministry of Japanese Finance, New Office Award, TBWA\HAKUHODO, Tokyo

2005

D&AD Award, Environmental Design & Architecture, Leaf Chapel, Kobuchizawa

2004

I.D. Annual Design Review, First Prize, Green Green Screen, Tokyo

2003

Architectural Record Award for Excellence in Design, Beacon Communications Office, Tokyo

Good Design Award, Beacon Communications Office, Tokyo

2002

Architectural Review, ar+d Emerging Architecture Award, First Prize, Pika Pika Pretzel, Tokyo

1997

Asahi Glass Design Award, Idée Workstation, Tokyo

1993

SD Review, Kajima Award, Exhibition of Winning Architectural Projects, Video Sento

Acknowledgments

It's that part of the book where acknowledgments are in order, yet our biggest fear is that we will miss someone! If you have read this far, then there is a very good chance you have been a part of our journey to Tokyo and Beyond, and we want to thank you first from the bottom of our hearts.

We do have to give a tip of the hat to Buzz Lightyear for the idea for the subtitle of the book, which is a play on "To Infinity and Beyond." It has been an incredible journey, and we want to thank Yukinari Hisayama for being with us for 30 of those years! Without him and all the Klein Dytham architecture allstars, there would be no KDa.

Architecture and design are very much about teamwork, with everyone playing their crucial part. Without our trusting clients, amazing structural engineers, patient MEP engineers, diligent construction companies and craftsmen, lush landscape designers, colorful graphic designers, and sharp photographers, there would be no awesome, iconic Klein Dytham architecture projects.

This monograph is itself an iconic project, brought to life over several years by an incredible team. A heartfelt thank you to the team at Images Publishing and to Honorine Le Fleur, a longtime friend who finally persuaded us to embark on this journey. Her generous guidance transformed what once seemed impossible into reality. Her team, including senior graphic designer Ryan Marshall and editor Helen Koehne, navigated the process with creativity, positivity, and remarkable patience. Mio Yamada, who first wrote about us in *The Japan Times*, took on the formidable task of writing about all seventy-six projects in this book, bringing architecture and design to life with her accessible and engaging style. But this book would not have taken flight without the extraordinary skill of KDa allstar Yuko Yoshikawa, who compiled, collaborated, organized, cajoled, and ultimately made it all happen. To each and every one of you on this remarkable team—our deepest gratitude.

Finally, we want to thank our families, and we have many. Our Deluxe, SuperDeluxe and Supernatural-Deluxe families are still vivid parts of our lives in Japan. For over 20 years, our ever-growing PechaKucha global family has amazed and humbled us daily. To have so many friends all around the world who share their creativity and passion makes all the effort of running this network worthwhile. Not a day goes by without getting a message to say PechaKucha has changed someone's career, life, or city.

And, of course, we have to thank our own families, who genuinely inspire us on our creative journeys and let us get away with this fantastic folly that we call architecture.

Photography Credits

Benny Chan: 135–7

Brian Scott Peterson: 91, 196–201, 303, 309 (top right), 318, 332–3

Chris Gascoigne: 130–3

Daici Ano: 77–9, 151–2, 168–9, 187–9, 229, 232–3, 259–60, 266–7, 272–3, 295–9

Graphics Factory CC / www.vectorworldmap.com: 12–13

Courtesy Hoshino Resorts RISONARE Atami: 203

Jun Takagi: 301

Katsuhisa Kida: 179–83, 191–3, 238–41, 263, 265, 284–5, 288–9, 291 (top), 292–3, 300

Courtesy Klein Dytham architecture: 21, 220–1, 253, 261, 278–9, 281–3, 286–7, 290, 291 (bottom), 306–7, 309 (top left, bottom left, bottom right), 317, 319

Ketsiree Wongwan: 99, 104–9

Ketsiree Wongwan / Corporation 4d Limited: 125, 127 (top)

Koichi Torimura: 84–5, 88–9, 128–9, 153–7, 204–5, 207–9, 219, 225–7, 247, 250–1, 255–7

Kozo Takayama: 148 (top), 158–9, 164–7, 230–1, 269–71

Makoto Yoshida: 195

Mark Dytham / Klein Dytham architecture: 26, 172–3, 185, 222–3, 248–9, 277, 305, 313–15

Michael Holmes: 320–3, 325

Nacása & Partners: cover, 10, 15–19, 23–5, 27–9, 31–5, 37–47, 49–51, 53–5, 57–65, 67–9, 80–3, 86–7, 93–7, 111–23, 139–43, 147, 148 (bottom), 149, 161–3, 171, 174–6, 243–5, 264, 275, 294

Petri Artturi Asikainen / Artek: 144–5

Ryota Atarashi: 235–7

Shingo Nakashima / SS Tokyo: 71–5

SpaceShift: 100–3

Takumi Ota: 211–17

Ujin Matsuo: 310–11

Weerapon Singnoi / Corporation 4d Limited: 126, 127 (bottom)

Published in Australia in 2025 by
The Images Publishing Group Pty Ltd
ABN 89 059 734 431

Offices

Melbourne
Waterman Business Centre
Suite 64, Level 2 UL40
1341 Dandenong Road
Chadstone, Victoria 3148
Australia
Tel: +61 3 8564 8122

New York
6 West 18th Street 4B
New York City, NY 10011
United States
Tel: +1 212 645 1111

Shanghai
6F, Building C, 838 Guangji Road
Hongkou District, Shanghai 200434
China
Tel: +86 021 31260822

books@imagespublishing.com
www.imagespublishing.com

The Images Publishing Group Reference Number: 1723

A catalogue record for this book is available from the National Library of Australia

Title: Klein Dytham architecture: to Tokyo and Beyond
Author: Astrid Klein and Mark Dytham
ISBN: 9781864709933

This title was commissioned in IMAGES' Melbourne office and produced as follows:
Graphic Design and Project Management Ryan Marshall; *Editorial* Rebecca Gross, Helen Koehne, Jeanette Wall; *Proofing* Andrea Dobbin; *Production* Simon Walsh, Heather Johnson; *Prepress* A & S Graphics (Singapore)

EU GPSR Authorised Representative: Easy Access System Europe Oü
Company Registration ID: 16879218 | Address: Mustamäe tee 50, 10621 Tallinn, Estonia
Email: gpsr@easproject.com | Tel: +358 40 500 3575

MIX
Paper | Supporting responsible forestry
FSC® C019910

Printed on 157gsm Chinese OJI FSC® matt art paper by Artron Art (Group) Co., Ltd, in China